GUIDING THE READING PROGRAM

A READING CONSULTANT'S HANDBOOK

H. Alan Robinson
The University of Chicago

Sidney J. Rauch
Hofstra University

With the assistance of

William Q. Davis, *Reading Consultant, Bensenville, Illinois*
Alverissa Miller, *Principal, Chesterton, Indiana*
Joan Ross, *Reading Consultant, Dolton, Illinois*

 Science Research Associates, Inc. Chicago
A Subsidiary of IBM

The word *handbook* may mean many different things. Obviously this little volume is not a compendium of existing knowledge on the state of reading instruction. Rather, it is an attempt to offer the reading consultant —and those who work with him—a series of operational guidelines which should help him function more effectively. The chief emphasis, therefore, is on how the reading consultant administers his duties—on what procedures he may follow and what functional aids he may employ in carrying on his work.

We hope this handbook will be helpful to inexperienced as well as to experienced reading consultants. Because knowledge of the field of reading instruction is presumed, the focus of the handbook is not on professional content, whether methods or materials. Instead we have attempted to describe and analyze the roles of the reading consultant in serving the community, school administrators, teachers, and members of the special services staff in the school system.

Because of its importance in the work of the reading consultant, the area of human relations is a special concern in this handbook. A person who does not relate well to many kinds of people will achieve limited success, at best, as a reading consultant. Although his primary task is to work with teachers, he must spread the concept that all members of the school and community team are working toward an improvement in reading instruction and helping each child move ever closer to his own reading potential. Only when the well-prepared consultant establishes warm relationships will he begin to reap the rewards of his profession.

Although the reading consultant is concerned with the overall reading program, including both developmental and remedial aspects, this handbook (with the exception of Chapter 6) deals primarily with the consultant's relationship to the developmental reading program. Beginning with an introduction, which delineates the various roles of the consultant, the handbook goes on, chapter by chapter, to relate these roles to specific situations. The rather lengthy Resources section closes the book with extensive bibliographies and lists of audio-visual materials, as well as special discussions of such topics as independent activities for the classroom and criteria for sound reading programs.

We hope that the ideas in the handbook will be of substantial help to reading consultants themselves as they work toward the improvement of reading instruction. However, the handbook should be useful reading for others seeking information about the roles of the reading consultant. Administrators may learn of the value of establishing a reading consultant's post in a school system now lacking one or, if one already exists, may be encouraged to work with the consultant toward a more precise and comprehensive definition of the position. Teachers reading the handbook may learn more about the variety of services rendered by the consultant—including, perhaps, many services of which they were previously unaware. Indeed, in many situations—for instance, in graduate courses training teachers as reading specialists—the handbook may be read to clarify the general design of the consultant's role in school.

The first draft of the handbook grew out of a two-week graduate Workshop in the Supervision of Reading Instruction held at Hofstra University, Hempstead, New York, in July 1960. We, the present authors, were privileged to direct this workshop. Participants in the workshop, consisting of reading consultants, supervisors, and administrators in the New York area, represented both elementary and secondary levels. Each of the participants listed below contributed ideas to the first draft.

*Berck, Lee	Molleson, Mary V.
Biederman, Theodore J.	Moses, Helen
Busteed, Grace	*Moss, Marion
Crinklaw, Frances	*Moynahan, Alice
*Demos, Lillian	O'Rourke, Kathleen
Dobrin, Ruth	Pampris, Chrysanthe
*Finsmith, Irene D.	Patterson, Ada
*Furedi, Ruth	Pavel, Adelaide
Garavente, Louis	*Ragger, Rita A.
*Gilles, Barbara	*Reis, Florence
*Gunter, Elizabeth	Schuler, Rose
Hall, Maxine	Tessier, Joseph H.
*Honikel, Eileen R.	Underwood, Alice
Hutto, Arueila	Wells, Ruth
Kooperstein, Rhoda	*Wile, Edith
Lansing, John E.	*Woodaman, Fleeta
Matises, Norma	

An editorial committee (composed of those persons whose names above are marked with asterisks) worked with us on a second draft during the latter part of 1960 and the spring of 1961. In 1962 we undertook the task of getting the material ready for publication.

We should especially like to acknowledge the efforts of William Q. Davis, Alverissa Miller, and Joan Ross for their great expenditure of time and skill in revising and adding to the second draft. Without their continuous cooperation, the authors could never have completed the volume. In addition, Carol Hostetter and Ann Preston Hayes, research assistants at the University of Chicago, are to be thanked for their bibliographical and editorial assistance.

Royalties earned from the sale of the handbook will be contributed, in equal proportions, to the Scholarship Fund of the Hofstra University Reading Center and to the William S. Gray Research Fund at the University of Chicago.

H. Alan Robinson
Sidney J. Rauch

CONTENTS

PREFACE

INTRODUCTION: Roles of the Reading Consultant 1

CHAPTER 1 RELATIONSHIPS WITH THE COMMUNITY 4
Relationships with the Board of Education 5
Relationships with Parents and Other Interested Adults 6
Informational Techniques 9
For further reading 11

CHAPTER 2 RELATIONSHIPS WITH ADMINISTRATORS 12
Mutual Areas of Interest 12
Reports 15
New Approaches to Reading Instruction 16
For further reading 24

CHAPTER 3 RELATIONSHIPS WITH TEACHERS 25
Evaluation 25
Classroom Organization 27
Materials 33
Observations and Interclass Visitations 34
Demonstrations 35
Research 36
Reading Committee 38
For further reading 38

CHAPTER 4 RELATIONSHIPS WITH OTHER MEMBERS OF
THE SCHOOL STAFF 39
Relationships with Curriculum and Supervision Specialists 39
Relationships with the Psychologist 42
Relationships with the Speech Specialist 43
Relationships with the School Nurse 44
Relationships with Guidance Personnel 44
Relationships with the School Librarian 45
Relationships with Nonprofessional Personnel 46
For further reading 46

CHAPTER 5 IN-SERVICE TRAINING 47
Orientation 48
When School Starts 49
As the Year Progresses 50
Establishing a Professional Library 55
For further reading 56

CHAPTER 6 REMEDIAL READING 57
Definition of the Retarded Reader 57
Identification of the Retarded Reader 57
Diagnosis of the Retarded Reader 59
Providing for Remedial Instruction 60
For further reading 63

CHAPTER 7 EVALUATION 64
Purposes of Evaluation 64
Tools of Evaluation 66
Criteria for the Selection of Standardized Tests 67
An Appraisal of Standardized Tests 68
Informal Measures 71
For further reading 75

RESOURCES

GUIDELINES FOR A GOOD READING PROGRAM 77
Criteria for a Sound Reading Program in the Elementary School . 77
Criteria for a Sound Reading Program in High School and
College 78
Reading Skills Checklist 78
Criteria for Selecting and Evaluating Reading Materials 80
Reading: How the Parent Can Help 81

INDEPENDENT ACTIVITIES FOR INDIVIDUALS OR SMALL
GROUPS 84

BIBLIOGRAPHIES 97
Books and Materials for Teachers of Reading 97
Selected Books and Materials for the Reading Consultant 100
Selected Books and Materials on Reading for Parents 103
List of Educational Publishers 105

AUDIO-VISUAL AIDS 108
Vocabulary 108
Comprehension 109
Reading Rate 110
Study Skills 111
Reference Aids 112
Word Recognition 113
General 115
Materials for In-Service Training 115
Selected Catalogs and Source Books of Audio-Visual Materials .. 116
List of Publishers of Audio-Visual Materials 117

INDEX 119

ROLES OF THE READING CONSULTANT

In our American schools, staff members assigned primarily to work with teachers in the improvement of reading instruction are frequently called *reading consultants*. Because the title seems most appropriate in terms of job description, *reading consultant* will be the designation used in this handbook. However, it should be noted that consultants are often known by other titles, most of them misleading. Because some consultants also conduct remedial and developmental reading classes, they have occasionally become known as "reading teachers," "remedial reading teachers," or "helping teachers"; but such titles are more appropriately reserved for those teachers with special training or for those wholly engaged in teaching reading under the direction of the consultant. In like fashion, other titles given to reading consultants tend to be ambiguous: "reading specialist" is too generic; "reading supervisor" connotes the conducting of activities concerned with teacher rating; "director of reading" or "reading coordinator" often refers to a top-level position which includes the supervision of the activities of consultants. In this handbook, therefore, a reading consultant is defined as a person largely freed of classroom teaching and other school responsibilities in order that he may concentrate on assisting the staff in the coordination and facilitation of efforts to improve the reading program.

The following is a list of the specific roles of the reading consultant as conceived in this handbook.

As a *resource person,* the reading consultant—
Supplies materials on request.
Helps select and evaluate materials, including tests.
Suggests methods appropriate to individual needs.
Answers questions about reading asked by staff members
and members of the community.

As an *adviser,* the reading consultant—
Advises administrators, teachers, and other members of the staff about
the teaching of reading within the school or school system.

Keeps the school staff up to date on new developments in reading as reflected in research reports, experimentation in other school districts, and reports at professional meetings.

Confers with parents, in order to interpret the school reading program or discuss individual problems.

As an *in-service leader,* the reading consultant—

Arranges for and occasionally teaches in-service courses in reading.

Conducts demonstration lessons in the classrooms of individual teachers or before groups of teachers.

Directs or arranges for short-term informal sessions, or workshops, in which groups of teachers may give specific attention to certain problems that arise in carrying out the instructional program in reading.

Plans and helps to implement the total school in-service program, especially those aspects which are directed toward the training of new teachers.

As an *investigator,* the reading consultant—

Encourages teachers to experiment with new materials and methods.

Designs research plans involving a group of teachers, the school, or the school system.

Reports the results of these research studies.

As a *diagnostician,* the reading consultant—

Directs or conducts diagnoses of individual students who appear to be severely retarded in reading.

Helps teachers learn to diagnose more effectively.

Interprets the results of diagnoses to staff members, to parents, and sometimes to the students themselves.

Attempts to help teachers, in regular classrooms or remedial situations, to make use of information from diagnoses in their teaching.

As an *instructor,* the reading consultant—

Helps teachers, formally and informally, to learn about methods and materials that will be useful to them.

Helps specific students at times, especially those very retarded in reading.

May teach a group (remedial or developmental) in order to try out new ideas or demonstrate certain procedures as a part of teacher training.

As an *evaluator,* the reading consultant—

Directs, supervises, or coordinates schoolwide testing programs involving reading achievement and capacity testing.

Interprets test results to the staff and community.

Investigates the curriculum and teaching procedures to ascertain ways of correcting faults demonstrated by test results.

Conducts, with the help of the total staff, complete periodical evaluations of the reading program.

Assists in the selection of new tests to be used in a school program.

In the chapters that follow, these various roles are discussed in fuller detail—chiefly in terms of the ways in which the reading consultant can win the confidence of parents, administrators, teachers, and other school officials and establish with them relationships of cooperation and harmony. Attention is also given to means of organizing such programs as in-service courses, remedial reading classes, and testing or evaluation systems. Indeed, *organizing* is the key word in these pages, for the focus is on the reading consultant as an organizer or coordinator of programs and personal relationships. The whole attempt is to suggest how—regardless of the specific reading approaches he chooses—the consultant may effectively execute desired policies and decisions.

CHAPTER 1

RELATIONSHIPS WITH THE COMMUNITY

The schools belong to the community, and it is as important for the school to know the community as it is for the community to understand the school. The exchange of information basic to such understanding can be facilitated by the perceptive reading consultant.

The new reading consultant or the reading consultant in a new situation can become familiar with the nature of his community through conversations with school personnel, examination of school board records, investigation of community and school surveys, and study of student records, as well as through the less formal means of observing and carefully reading the local newspaper. Community attitudes toward the reading program and toward reading instruction in general may differ widely. The consultant should be as familiar with these attitudes as he is with such matters as socioeconomic levels and the number of community graduates going to college. The reading consultant must maintain an active interest in discovering and appraising the atmosphere of the community throughout his tenure of office. To "sell" the reading program to the community, the consultant must be well versed in what, how, and why things are done both in the community and in the school.

The reading consultant is also responsible for appraising resources in the community. He will want to learn about the possibilities of interrelationships between the reading program and medical, psychological, and guidance resources in the community. He should meet with the people engaged in such specialties to explain the reading program and to find out how sympathetic as well as how knowledgeable they are. He will also want to investigate referral opportunities both in related disciplines and in reading itself. College and private reading clinics should be visited and evaluated *prior to referral.*

Obviously the reading consultant, if he is to communicate with members of the community, must have a thorough knowledge of the reading program as it exists in the schools of the community. He must know its strengths and its weaknesses as well as its goals. He must know the present status of the program and be able to present the statistics and other facts which validate his conclusions.

Communication with members of the community must be carefully planned; in communication, confusion leads to friction and understanding leads to cooperation. Public opinion must not be left to shift for itself. The reading consultant must give constant attention to helping the public move toward a fuller appreciation of the problems and goals of the reading program.

Relationships with the Board of Education

The board of education must be kept constantly informed of plans and procedures concerning the reading program, so that it will lend its full support to each phase of development. The reading consultant should develop and maintain a systematic means of communicating with the board.

Communication can take the following forms:

REPORTS. The consultant may wish to report on any or all of the following: new developments and proposed developments in the reading program, conferences (planned, attended, or held), reading research going on in the local system, other reading research affecting the local reading program, and evaluations of the reading program. The reports, of course, should be cleared in advance with the principal or superintendent—in accordance with school policy.

TIPS

PREPARATION OF REPORTS TO THE BOARD OF EDUCATION

1. Base generalizations on verifiable data.
2. Use audio-visual aids in oral reports whenever feasible.
3. Follow up oral reports with written reports. In such reports try to avoid educational jargon and define essential terms.
4. Use graphic materials in written reports when applicable.
5. Deliver and write reports with the personalities and understandings of the board members in mind.
6. With each key report, prepare a summary for those board members who do not have the time or the desire to wade through complicated data.

INVITATIONS. Board members should be encouraged to observe the reading program in progress. If the reading consultant wishes to highlight a particular phase of the developmental or remedial program, special invitations should be issued.

COMMUNITY AND SCHOOL FUNCTIONS. The reading consultant should take every opportunity to participate in social functions through which he may become better acquainted with the members of the school board.

Relationships with Parents and Other Interested Adults

KINDERGARTEN ORIENTATION. A valuable orientation for parents will include a tour, with explanation and discussion, covering the readiness program in kindergarten—that is, the whys and hows of a kindergarten program. To ensure success, the reading consultant should help the kindergarten teachers prepare materials and explanations to be presented to parents. A major point to be covered is the importance of the home to the child's success in reading, both before the child enters school and as he continues through the grades. The orientation program should be supplemented with take-home materials for later digestion and reference.

PARENT-TEACHING DAY. Having parents teach a specific reading lesson has been tried with great success in a number of situations. It is an effective means of enabling parents to understand the many problems faced by the teacher. But careful planning is essential. The reading consultant should hold orientation meetings and arrange for parents to receive manuals and materials in advance. Reasons for using specific methods should be explained if lesson plans call for such methods. It is also important that a general follow-up meeting be scheduled after the "Day."

PARENT CONFERENCES. Although the reading consultant may need to see individual parents from time to time, generally his major function is to help the teachers prepare for parent conferences, especially when reading is to be discussed. The reading consultant might help arrange schedules to facilitate the visit, especially when parents must see both classroom teachers and a reading teacher. The reading consultant should also advise teachers to see parents early in the school year, so that problems may be aired and solutions viewed. Parents have every right to be annoyed if not informed for many months that their child is failing in reading or that a reading disability appears to be causing failures in the content areas.

Teachers must understand the reading program if they are to communicate effectively with parents. The reading consultant can provide this overall understanding by meeting with groups of teachers or consulting with individual teachers *prior* to the actual conferences. He should particularly address himself to new teachers just out of college, teachers new to the school or the school system, and teachers needing aid because of unhappy experiences in holding parent-teacher conferences in the past. And he should impress upon these teachers the need to employ the following approaches to the parents at the conference.

1. *Prepare carefully for the conference.* Assemble a file of pertinent samples of the student's work related to reading activities. Review anecdotal records and data in the student's cumulative folder. Evaluate recent test results in the light of student performance and ability. Contact other teachers for their observations of the student.

2. *Be a good listener.* Use part of the conference, especially the first part, to learn about the student from the parent. Much important information about interests and reading habits can be gained in this way. On the other hand, the parent comes to realize that the teacher is interested in his child and the child's family.

3. *Answer questions completely.* Make answers as concrete as possible. Let suggestions for specific solutions to problems grow out of mutual discussion.

4. *Be tactful, but realistic.* If a student is reading about three years below expectancy level, say so. Evasion or the glossing over of facts will only result in poor public relations at some other time. The student can be severely hurt if attention is not focused early on his specific needs.

5. *Ask the parent for help.* Parents are usually pleased to cooperate and especially gratified to know the teacher wants their help. They may be able to offer help with certain problems related to attitudes or even to performance in reading.

6. *Be positive.* Be sure the parent understands your major points. Begin and end the conference with positive rather than negative comments.

7. *Keep the vocabulary simple.* The goal is understanding. Technical terms such as "consonant blends," "rate of comprehension," and "inference questions" should be explained, if used.

8. *Invite parents to observe reading lessons.* Such visits should be planned beforehand and followed by a discussion. These personal observations are particularly important when parents indicate a lack of understanding of particular aspects of the reading program.

COMMUNITY-SCHOOL JOINT ENTERPRISE. Parents and other interested adults in the community may join the professional faculty in conducting a survey of reading services in the school or school system. They may also have representation on curriculum-planning committees or other groups organized to survey the status quo and to investigate the need for change. A joint effort like this furthers understanding and helps to block the "action faction" who have seen only what is wrong and have failed to see the total picture. Certain adults and students may make effective members of an ongoing reading committee dedicated to improving reading instruction.

Under some circumstances an alternative to joint parent-teacher committeeship is advisable. Adults and perhaps students in the community might be encouraged to maintain their own independent committee, which feeds its findings as suggestions to the professional group. Either plan is feasible—joint committees or independent but coordinated committees.

Parents and students can also be useful as reading tutors. Several large cities have organized programs in which parents and topnotch high school and college students work with individual students in need of reading help. A reading consultant can assist a great deal by serving as a trainer and adviser. Brief workshops for the people engaged in this tutoring, as well as for parents interested in helping their own children, can be extremely helpful if well planned and administered.

PARENT-TEACHER ASSOCIATIONS. The reading consultant should be an active member of the Parent-Teacher Association, an agency with the potential to offer positive action and active support provided its members understand the reading program and are informed of weaknesses, strengths, changes, and goals. The PTA can help to raise money for necessary materials or equipment not budgeted but, nevertheless, urgently needed. It can also help to raise money for referrals—that is, for students who need outside help but whose families are financially unable to pay for the services of a tutor or reading clinic.

SUMMER ACTIVITIES. The reading program does not terminate with the close of the school year. A continued interest in reading should be fostered, and opportunities to utilize reading skills should be provided during the summer months.

Prior to the close of school the consultant may meet with parents to plan summer reading programs for their children. If no *formal* summer reading program exists, the consultant may want to provide certain parents with referral lists of teachers skilled in the teaching of developmental or remedial reading. Or before the end of the school year, teachers, with the help of the reading consultant, may provide parents with book lists suitable for a variety of interests and reading levels. If a formal summer program does exist, parents should be encouraged to enroll their children for the needed instruction.

In addition to the summer reading program, the consultant will want to offer parents information about other facilities available to their children during the summer months: information about the daily hours of the community library, the story-hour activities at the library, the visits of bookmobiles, the language arts programs in nearby communities or in other local institutions, and the camps that have reading programs. The reading consultant should encourage school libraries to remain open during the summer, and he should enlist parents' help in getting their children to use the library facilities.

Informational Techniques

(To communicate effectively with the community at large, as well as with individuals in the community, the reading consultant should use a variety of communication methods. The materials and techniques listed in the discussion that follows are widely employed, and successful reading consultants obtain best results by using several means of communication concurrently.

① PRINTED MATERIALS. (Three types of printed material may be usefully distributed. First, there are the pamphlets and bulletins on such topics as "Questions You've Asked About Reading Instruction," "How Does a Child First Learn to Read?" and "Reading Skills and Mathematics." (See the Resources section for other suggestions and for sources of information.) These materials should be easy to read and yet as specific as possible; educational jargon should be avoided, but if technical terms must be used, they should be carefully defined. Most important, the materials should be distributed at the time when they are most needed. For example, parents about to send a child to kindergarten or grade 1 can be saved a great deal of anxiety if they can learn something early about reading readiness and about what to expect of the child. A conference alone is not sufficient to alleviate this problem.

② A second type of useful printed material is the form letter regarding remedial referrals, conferences, or progress reports; such letters should be distributed to parents as occasion demands.

③ Book lists, the third type of printed material, should be geared to reading and interest levels. Their distribution can be handled at grade-level meetings, book fairs, PTA meetings, and the local library.

EXHIBITS AND DISPLAYS. (Visual aids—in the form of exhibits and displays—are an excellent means of communicating with the public, and a variety of locations for the exhibits are possible: public meeting places, book fairs, shop windows, community libraries, and bulletin boards. Some consultants have also selected nights for open house or have promoted traveling exhibits in order to reach the widest possible audience. The materials that may be displayed are various:

Specific textbooks and workbooks used in the program
Instruments of various kinds used in the program
Multilevel materials
Homemade and commercial reading games
Tradebooks clustered about an interesting theme
Experience charts and stories
Items showing the results of individual or class projects
Magazine articles, cartoons, and newspaper clippings highlighting certain aspects of a reading program
Artwork and book reports emanating from the student's reading

MOVIES AND SLIDES. Any of the periodic conferences, book fairs, and other gatherings already noted may be the occasion for the showing of movies and slides. See the Resources section for offerings currently available from various institutions and film distributors.

COLLEGE- OR SCHOOL-SPONSORED COURSES. The reading consultant should be instrumental in bringing educators from local colleges into contact with members of the community. Evening college courses or adult education courses may help parents and other taxpayers to understand how reading is currently taught in schools and how parents can offer guidance at home.

THE PRESS. One of the reading consultant's greatest informational opportunities is offered by the news media in general and the commercial newspaper in particular. It is up to the reading consultant and the administration to develop a smooth working relationship with the press, for only through mutual understanding between school and press can the consultant secure an accurate reporting of school news and ward off the possibility of distorted facts being presented to the public. In some situations the reading consultant will work through another school official charged with the responsibility of public relations. But should the reading consultant be directly responsible to the press and other news media, he should constantly examine his reading program with a fresh perspective. To reporters he can then continually supply fresh information about representative classroom activities and about the whys of various methods and activities. A good channel for this information is the newsletter sent out by the school to the various media. If he demonstrates responsibility, the consultant may be invited by the local newspaper to contribute directly to its feature columns on schools and education.

LESSON DEMONSTRATIONS. The community should be given the opportunity to observe the reading program in progress. One method is to invite parents and other interested adults to a series of carefully planned lesson demonstrations in classrooms representing all grade levels (primary, intermediate, junior high, senior high).

The reading consultant must play a major role in the planning and execution of such a project. The planning itself may take a year or more and should be undertaken by a reading committee representing all levels and subject areas. (For information on staging lesson demonstrations, consult H. Alan Robinson *et al.,* "Does Your Community Know Your Reading Program?" *Journal of Developmental Reading,* I [Autumn 1957], 7–16.)

PANEL DISCUSSIONS. Panelists may be scheduled to speak immediately following a demonstration or talk, or their discussion may actually constitute a program in itself. The choice of topics is large—for example, "Help-

---

TIPS

PREPARATION OF LESSON DEMONSTRATIONS

1. Before the demonstration, acquaint the audience with the overall objectives of the reading program.
2. Indicate what has happened prior to the lesson they will observe and what will follow it.
3. Distribute copies of the material to be used by the students during the lesson.
4. Be sure the demonstration is carefully planned and executed by a master teacher and showman.
5. Encourage discussion, and answer questions objectively in simple language *after* the students in the demonstration have been dismissed.
6. Have the audience fill out specific evaluation sheets.
7. Have an exhibit of materials available for examination.
8. Encourage those present to come to the school for planned follow-up observations.

---

ing the Child Learn to Read," "What Has Helped Us Most with Our Reading," or "How We Learned to Read."

MEETINGS. Reading consultants are sometimes called before public meetings, especially PTA meetings, to report on and discuss facets of the school's reading program. In order to elicit maximum interest and understanding, the consultant must be sure that his presentation is geared to the audience. He must exhibit real interest in his subject, speak positively and in lay terms, and be sure that any other participants in the program are well prepared.

Presentations should be specific, limited in scope, and concerned with concrete matters. Explanations of difficult or detailed concepts should be printed or mimeographed and distributed to members of the audience.

FOR FURTHER READING

Development in and through Reading. (60th Yearbook of the National Society for the Study of Education, Part I.) Chicago: Univ. of Chicago Press, 1961. Chap. 6.

NEWTON, J. ROY. *Reading in Your School.* New York: McGraw-Hill, 1960. Chap. 10.

UMANS, SHELLEY. *New Trends in Reading Instruction.* New York: Bureau of Publications, Teachers College, Columbia Univ., 1963. Chap. 5.

CHAPTER **2**

RELATIONSHIPS WITH ADMINISTRATORS

The administrator delegates certain responsibilities to the reading consultant; hence he must maintain a constant and continuing interest in the activities of the reading consultant. Together the administrator and the consultant must clarify the multiple facets of the consultant's role, as well as the administrator's role in relation to the reading program. Depending on the nature and size of the school system, the consultant may be responsible directly to the superintendent or to a building principal. Most often he is employed at a district level and is responsible to the superintendent, although he works through the principal of each school.

Before the reading consultant accepts a position, he should help ensure ultimate success by defining with the administrator the nature of the position —its scope as well as its limitations. It is vital that the administrator view reading as an intrinsic part of the curriculum and that he be willing actively and publicly to support the activities of the reading consultant. In fact, as they both try to meet objectives, the consultant has the right to expect that the administrator be familiar with the objectives and practices of the reading program and with the behavior of his school population. He even has a right to expect that the administrator endeavor to select classroom teachers who love children and books and are knowledgeable about teaching reading.

On his part, the reading consultant should be prepared to answer any questions that the administrator might ask about reading instruction and theory. Administrators should not hire consultants who do not meet at least the *Minimum Standards for Professional Training of Reading Specialists* developed by the International Reading Association. Since these minimum standards are of immediate and practical concern to both administrators and reading consultants, they are described in detail at the end of this chapter. It is important that administrators be familiar with these standards when interviewing prospective candidates for the position of reading consultant.

Mutual Areas of Interest

Agreement between the reading consultant and the administrator on the points discussed below will help ensure mutual understanding.

12

LINE AND STAFF. Line and staff responsibilities should be clarified so that the consultant may be sure of his relative position in the chain of command. It is essential to the success of the reading program that the reading consultant be able to concentrate wholly on performing his own multiple duties. He should not be expected to take on responsibilities of teacher evaluation. On the other hand, he should not be considered someone who can easily function as a fill-in merely because he has no direct involvement in classroom instruction or in school administration. The reading consultant guides the reading program; he is not a floating substitute or school aide who takes over classes on the spur of the moment, acts as proctor in an extra study hall, or assumes semipermanent lunchroom duty.

The *status* of the reading consultant is an important consideration. If educational administrators believe that the task of improving reading on a schoolwide basis is indeed of major importance, then they must see that the person who assumes primary responsibility for this job is recognized and rewarded—as a specialized professional. To be considered a substitute teacher or a general school aide will detract considerably from the reading consultant's status. In many cases such treatment will reduce his effectiveness in working with and guiding the regular classroom teacher toward better reading instruction.

MECHANICS. To facilitate the mechanical aspects of the reading program, the reading consultant should—

1. Discover methods for exchanging information related to the reading program and establish criteria for judging what is to be brought to the administrator's attention.

2. Establish who should be responsible for supplying information to the school board, the press, the community, parents, and various school personnel.

3. Determine the availability of the administrator for meetings with other school personnel and attempt to find ways to avoid conflicts in the dates of meetings, so that the administrator can attend.

4. Determine a policy regarding attendance at institutes and conventions.

5. Ascertain procedures for ordering materials.

SCHEDULE. The reading consultant should convince administrators (who in turn should try to convince their staff members) that the job of the reading consultant calls for a flexible schedule. Such a flexible schedule is particularly important for the reading consultant who must serve more than one school. He must be free to determine the amount of time he will spend in each school, based on his evaluation of needs.

It is equally important that the consultant and the administrator agree on the areas to be emphasized in the job of the consultant. They should agree on the relative amount of time the reading consultant will spend on working with teachers, on teaching reading (certainly teaching duties should be limited and performed only if essential), on conducting workshops and other in-service activities, on keeping records, on taking inventory, on ordering and distributing supplies and materials, and, finally, on testing.

TIPS

CHECKLIST FOR CONSULTANTS

1. Do you see to it that your administrators are the first to know about new approaches and about plans for introducing a new program or a new teaching method, for giving a demonstration lesson, for sending bulletins to teachers or parents, for publishing articles you have written?

2. Do you send your administrator a note telling him of an exceptionally good reading lesson presented by one of the classroom teachers?

3. Do you preview professional magazines and other periodicals, making marginal notes, underlining, or duplicating highlights for the administrator?

4. Do you give your administrator recognition when he participates in some specific reading activity?

5. Do you make yourself available to serve on school committees and then dig in to do a good job?

6. Do you use an agenda for your scheduled meetings with the administrator? Do you send a copy of this agenda to the administrator prior to the meeting?

7. Do you have your reading meetings scheduled regularly with other school personnel? Do you have the principal's secretary put these dates on his calendar weeks ahead? Do you keep him up to date with reports of these meetings?

8. When working with an administrator, do you keep in mind that reading is only one important phase of the unified school program?

9. Do you recognize the community pressures or responsibilities that the administrator must consider as he evaluates your suggestions or proposals?

10. Most important, do you recognize the need for good human relations in building the best possible reading program?

BUDGET AND PLANT FACILITIES. The reading consultant should seek agreement on a sufficient budget for all aspects of the reading program. He should anticipate possible budget increases as the program expands; and in planning for both present and future needs, he should consider the costs of clerical assistance, materials and supplies, and additional professional personnel. Also to be determined are the school's or the system's physical needs, such as classroom space, office space, and storage facilities.

IN-SERVICE PROGRAMS. The consultant should determine the scope of the in-service program in reading and its possible development over a period of time. He should project a budget for the in-service program, but only after determining what system-owned materials are available. Every effort should be made to clarify the ways in which the in-service program in reading relates to other in-service activities.

POLICIES AND PRACTICES. The administrator and the consultant should clarify various school policies and practices affecting the reading program— that is, policies and practices involving homogeneous or other special groupings, promotions, reports to parents, testing, and textbook adoptions. Of course the administration should be made aware that policies and practices may occasionally require revision in the interests of the reading program.

SPECIAL SERVICES. Services involving guidance, health, psychological aid, and speech correction are available in many school systems. The consultant should determine which of these special services is available in his school system and how they relate to the reading program.

Reports

The reading consultant should prepare an annual report for the superintendent or the principal or for both—a report that summarizes the year's activities and makes recommendations for changes. Such a report might contain test results with the analyses of scores in terms of the particular school system. Budget needs should always be included. This is also a good opportunity to report the results of research and new ideas about reading instruction. The excerpt below has been adapted from the report to a superintendent made by one reading consultant.

> *Programed instruction in reading.* After spending the previous year examining materials, visiting schools using programs, and evaluating pros and cons, the reading committee decided to try one beginning reading program, since Mrs. Jones seemed particularly willing to experiment. Mrs. Jones's pupils did as well in reading as the twenty-two pupils who were matched with them but scattered around in other classrooms within one district. Hence this experimentation in programing reading instruction did not seem to get better results than our conventional programs. Mrs. Jones did

report that some of the better readers got so bored that she felt they would begin to dislike reading in general. This does not really seem to be the case, however; neither the better readers nor other groups seem to have developed a significant dislike for reading.

No decision has been made about further use of programed material for teaching reading. Miss Wilcox wants to try the same program with her very slow children.

A reading consultant working at the junior high school level concluded his report with the following:

ADDITIONAL SERVICES PROVIDED BY THE READING CONSULTANT

1. Submitted the budget for remedial reading department.
2. Submitted the budget for the supplementary textbooks and materials used in the seventh and eighth grades.
3. Administered individual and group tests.
4. Held conferences with teachers and parents on the reading program in the junior high school.
5. Attended three educational conferences on reading and curriculum development, and submitted reports to the superintendent.
6. Prepared an annotated bibliography for use of content-area teachers.
7. Supplied specially typed reading skills materials to teachers.
8. Organized a Teen-Age Book Club.
9. Arranged for six demonstration lessons involving the content areas.
10. Arranged for three demonstration lessons conducted by representatives of three major publishing companies.

The consultant may also prepare reports on special occasions, depending upon requests made by principals or the superintendent.

New Approaches to Reading Instruction

One of the primary responsibilities of the reading consultant is to be aware of new approaches or methods in the teaching of reading and to pass this information on to the administrator. Since these are times of ferment and experimentation in the reading field, most of our communications media have reported or are interested in reporting new approaches. However, some of the magazine and newspaper articles and the radio and television programs seem to be primarily concerned with new breakthroughs or cure-alls for our reading ills. The sensational is frequently highlighted, and a limited and informal experiment may eventually appear in print as a nation-wide success. Many parents base their questions and comments on these journal articles or programs on the air. They want to know what their schools are doing to take advantage of these new approaches. Frequently they will use press reports to criticize the present reading program.

In order to discuss and evaluate these methods intelligently, the reading consultant is presented here with brief summaries of five of the major "new" approaches. Each summary closes with further references.[1]

THE INITIAL TEACHING ALPHABET. Although there are a variety of methods of teaching reading, they all have one thing in common: the traditional English alphabet and spelling. It has been suggested that it is this traditional orthography which results in a large proportion of reading failures, no matter which of the current methods of teaching is being used. Sir James Pitman advocates the use of an Initial Teaching Alphabet (ITA) to remove the inconsistencies between sound and symbol. This alphabet is meant to be used only for beginning reading instruction, until the pupil is ready to make the transition to the traditional alphabet.

This alphabet, which was originally called the Augmented Roman Alphabet, has forty-four lowercase characters, twenty-four of them conventional letters. There are fourteen digraphs; the letters Q and X are omitted (because they do not have their own sound values); and the remainder of the letters have new configurations. Each symbol in ITA, according to Pitman, has one phonic meaning instead of the ambiguous phonic meanings of the symbols of traditional orthography. Only one printed form is used for each whole word. Thus a single visual pattern is presented to the child. The top halves of ITA characters have been kept as similar as possible to the top halves of corresponding traditional orthographic characters in order to facilitate transfer. Transition is made when each individual appears ready. Each pupil progresses through the reading program at his own pace and moves on to traditional orthography books when he has satisfactorily completed the course of ITA reading materials.

Although ITA brings about changes in the traditional spelling in its attempts to achieve greater simplicity and regularity, it is only the beginning step on the child's road to understanding traditional orthography. This ITA alphabet is to be discarded when pupils no longer appear to need it. Present evidence indicates that future research is expected not only in beginning reading instruction but also in the application of ITA to the problem of adult illiteracy and to serious remedial problems.

REFERENCES

DOWNING, JOHN. *Experiments with an Augmented Alphabet for Beginning Readers.* New York: Educational Records Bureau, 1962.

[1]This section was prepared with the assistance of Mrs. Judith Goodman, reading consultant, the Lawrence School, Hewlett, New York. Chapter 5 of Nila Banton Smith's *Reading Instruction for Today's Youth* (Englewood Cliffs, N.J.: Prentice-Hall, 1962) was the primary reference.

TANYZER, HAROLD J., and MAZURKIEWICZ, ALBERT J. *Early-to-Read i/t/a Series.* New York: Pitman's I.T.A. Publications, 1963.

THE PROGRAMED READING APPROACH. The programed instruction (or programed learning) approach analyzes a subject into its component parts and arranges the parts into a sequential learning order. At each step the student is expected to make a response, which may or may not be a written response. According to one theory of programed instruction, the program should be constructed so that incorrect answers will be held to a minimum; the resultant high percentage of correct responses is thought to reinforce the learning process.

Programed material may take the form of workbooks, textbooks, cards, or separate worksheets. It may also be presented in a variety of so-called teaching machines. The teaching machine as such does not and cannot teach; it is simply a device for presenting the small learning units, which are arranged in a logical, sequential order of instruction. It does have the advantage of preventing premature exposure of the correct response, thus forcing the student to concentrate on making his own response without "peeking." But this advantage may be outweighed by the flexibility of printed materials.

Programed instruction in reading may be useful—at least so it appears at its present stage of development—with concepts that need to be fixed, facts that need to be memorized, and processes that should be made automatic or habitual. It may prove to be an effective way of freeing the classroom teacher from drill work and its correction. Some attempts have been made to strengthen the traditional word-attack and other reading skills, and even to develop a critical approach to the reading of literary selections, through programed instruction.

REFERENCES

DETERLINE, WILLIAM A. *An Introduction to Programed Instruction.* Englewood Cliffs, N.J.: Prentice-Hall, 1962.

GREEN, EDWARD J. *The Learning Process and Programmed Instruction.* New York: Holt, Rinehart & Winston, 1962.

MARGULIES, STUART, and EIGAN, LEWIS D. *Applied Programmed Instruction.* New York: Wiley, 1962.

SULLIVAN, M. W., and BUCHANAN, CYNTHIA D. *Programmed Reading Series.* New York: McGraw-Hill, 1963.

THE LINGUISTICS APPROACH. Linguistics, the scientific study of language, focuses chiefly on the sound systems of language and the grammatical structures of language. Structural linguists, in analyzing language, are concerned especially with the patterning or ordering of words into phrases and sentences, with the form or morphology of words, and with the intonation patterns of speech ("terminals" or pauses, "junctures" or the transitions between words, and "stress" or the accenting of syllables).

Until recently, the nearest that reading instruction came to a linguistics approach was teaching of *phonics,* the reading method in which the beginning reader learns the "phonetic value" of letters of the alphabet, groups of letters, and syllables. However, linguists have pointed out that letters themselves do not have sounds; they are not "pronounced." Rather it is oral speech that is composed of sounds, and these sounds are then represented—in English, with some irregularity—by various letters of the alphabet. Because they feel that misconceptions about alphabets and speech sounds do exist, especially in the teaching of phonics, a few linguists have proposed that the vocabulary of beginning textbooks in reading include only those words that show a regular correspondence between letter and sound (grapheme and phoneme). During initial reading instruction, concentration would be placed on single, regularly spelled words—the belief being that irregulars should be held in abeyance as much as possible so that the beginning reader can systematically master the "regular" graphemic elements of the English language.

Other linguists have been less concerned with the problem of graphemic-phonemic correspondence than with the problem of transferring a child's understanding of how to "talk" to an understanding of how to "read" what he talks. In learning to talk, the preschool child has already learned certain simple grammatical signals; he knows that the group of words, "He isn't very nice to me," makes sense and that "He not to me very nice is" does not make sense, or, at least, is somehow wrong. These linguists feel that the child, as his experience grows, will continue to develop his understanding of how to distinguish and control more complex grammatical signals. But at the beginning, when the child is just learning to read—to recognize how "talk" is transferred into graphemic symbols—his attention should be kept concentrated on this transfer process. The structure and style of his textbook language should be similar to the structure and style of the spoken language he already knows, and instruction should emphasize the teaching of sentences rather than individual words or sounds. Later, after this initial "transfer stage" between talking and reading, the child may be led into reading that is more sophisticated than his speech.

The linguist has provided help in the teaching of reading, perhaps not so much by advocating a particular method as by identifying major similarities and differences in the alphabetical system and by studying the grammatical structure of the child's "home" and "school" language.

REFERENCES

FRIES, C. C. *Linguistics and Reading.* New York: Holt, Rinehart & Winston. 1963.

LEFEVRE, CARL. *Linguistics and the Teaching of Reading.* New York: McGraw-Hill, 1964.

SMITH, HENRY L., and STRATEMEYER, CLARA. *Linguistic Science Readers.* New York: Harper & Row, 1963.

THE MONTESSORI METHOD. It hardly seems fair to the adherents of the Montessori method to describe it as a new approach. The English edition of Maria Montessori's classic work, *The Montessori Method,* appeared in 1912, and her contributions to early childhood education have been discussed for decades. It is considered a "new approach" in this section because of the interest in and the publicity given to the Whitby School of Greenwich, Connecticut, the nation's first "pure" Montessori school.

The Montessori method was named after Maria Montessori, a graduate physician who in the late nineteenth century founded a school for slow-learning children in Rome and later applied her theories of education to normal and superior children aged three to six. In 1929 the International Montessori Society was founded. Although the Montessori method is not as well known in the United States as it is in Europe, many private schools in this country have adopted it for nursery, kindergarten, and first-grade children; some schools plan to continue with similar methods throughout the grades, as has the Whitby School.

In his recent book *The Montessori Method,* E. Mortimer Standing discussed the following fundamental Montessori principles:[2]

1. It is a method based on the principle of freedom in a prepared environment.

2. The child is in a state of continuous and intense transformation, of both body and mind, whereas the adult has reached the norm of the species.

3. The teacher (and parent) must guard, with unceasing vigilance, against any unnecessary interference with the child's work. Every useless aid we give to the child arrests his development. In this sense, Dr. Montessori prefers the word *directress* to *teacher* because her job is not so much to teach directly as to direct the child's continual supply of spontaneous mental energy into self-creative channels.

4. The child's intellect is sufficient—through its own *spontaneous* activity— to drive him on to acquire the elements of culture. We must make use of his sense of exploring, experimenting, and discovering.

5. Carefully graded sensory materials such as color tablets, rods, cylinders, cubes, and prisms set in order the child's past experiences and unlock new ones. The correct use and sequence of these "didactic materials" is essential.

[2]E. Mortimer Standing, *The Montessori Method* (Fresno, Calif.: Academy Library Guild. 1962), Chap. 1.

Thus, in the Montessori method, mental concepts are built by a carefully constructed sequence of experiences that proceed from concrete to abstract. Experience is gained through a "prepared environment" using specially constructed materials. These materials—particularly those related to the teaching of reading—include an alphabet of three-dimensional letters that can be manipulated by the child, sandpaper letters to feel and trace, and a variety of trade books and readers. The tactile approach is emphasized at first, but strong emphasis is also placed on oral language experiences. The teacher does a good deal of oral reading and leads the class in oral discussion before new words are introduced.

REFERENCES

FISHER, DOROTHY CANFIELD. *A Montessori Mother.* New York: Holt, 1912.

MONTESSORI, MARIA. *The Montessori Method.* New York: Frederick A. Stokes, 1912.

RAMBUSCH, NANCY M. *Learning How to Learn: An American Approach to Montessori.* Baltimore, Helicon Press, 1962.

STANDING, E. MORTIMER. *The Montessori Method.* Fresno, Calif.: Academy Library Guild, 1962.

THE LANGUAGE-EXPERIENCE APPROACH. The language-experience approach has received much momentum from its use in the schools of San Diego County, California. It is not a new approach but rather an outgrowth and enrichment of the widely used experience chart technique. Reading and other communication skills are brought together in the instructional program from the first day in school. The teacher provides opportunities for each child to improve his language power by sharing his ideas with others through the use of words and pictures. The teacher records the child's oral stories in summary form on his pictures. The child then "reads" his stories to the class. The stories continue to serve as the basic reading materials for all children until such time as their sight vocabularies are developed sufficiently to read preprimers and other easy books. During this period word ladders, picture dictionaries, labels, and stories the teacher may read or tell to the children are used to strengthen the children's skills in word recognition and interpretation.

The teacher may work with the individual child or with the whole group as he records the stories. He calls attention to letter formation, the relation of beginning sounds to the symbols used, repetition of sound and symbol in many situations, capitalization, punctuation, and sentence meanings. Within a short time children appear to write their own stories independently. Gradually they acquire increased competence in reading. The language-experience approach places emphasis upon the communication skills, creative writing, storytelling, discussions, and listening.

REFERENCES

ALLEN, VAN R., and LEE, DORIS MAY. *Learning to Read Through Experience.*
New York: Appleton-Century-Crofts, 1963.

Description of Three Approaches to the Teaching of Reading. San Diego: San
Diego County Superintendent of Schools, 1962.

COLOR CODING. The newest of the new approaches attempting to solve
the reading problem appears to be the "words in color" method devised
by Caleb Gattegno, whose previous reputation rested mainly upon his
introduction of the Cuisenaire rods into the primary grades to teach mathe-
matical concepts and reasoning. Using a system of color-coded sounds, he
has applied a specific color to each of twenty vowel sounds, as well as twen-
ty-seven colors to the consonant sounds. Thus, the short *a* sound will be
printed in white, the short *u* in yellow, the short *i* in red, the short *e* in light
blue, and the short *o* in orange. According to Dr. Gattegno, "Since the in-
tention is to make English a phonetic language without altering the spelling
of English words, we have used color to differentiate among the sounds, using the same color for the same sound, regardless of the spelling, and
different colors for the same sign when it sounds differently. Thus, the *ay* in
w*ay*, the *eigh* in w*eigh,* the *ai* in w*ai*t, and the *a* in w*a*ne are all considered to
belong to the same sign group. They have one sound and, hence, one color
only."[3]

In Book 1, students first learn the short vowel sounds, then the consonants *f, t,* and *s.* In beginning instruction each sign is referred to by its color
instead of by its sound or name (twenty-one color charts are used in the
program). The term *visual dictation* is used to describe the blending of these
color sounds into various combinations, which sometimes produce English
words along with the many syllable sounds. Pupils discover new words. As
the pupils acquire a surer grasp of the words, sentences and stories are introduced. Although the use of color appears to be the distinctive feature of this
approach, its main purpose is to introduce and reinforce the pupil's mental
image of the sound-sign relationship. Dr. Gattegno emphasizes, "The most
distinctive characteristic of our approach is not so much the use of color to
make a language quasi-phonetic, but in the fact that this method uses the
dynamic properties of the mind."[4]

REFERENCES

GATTEGNO, CALEB. *Words in Color: Background and Principles.* Chicago: Learning Materials, Inc., 1962.

"Reading by Rainbow," *Time,* LXXXII (June 12, 1964), 59–60.

[3]Caleb Gattegno, *Words in Color* (Chicago: Learning Materials, Inc., 1962), p. 40.
[4]*Ibid.,* p. 10.

Minimum Standards for Professional Training of Reading Specialists[5]

I. A minimum of three years of successful teaching and/or clinical experience.

II. A master's degree or its equivalent of a bachelor's degree and 30 graduate hours in reading and related areas as indicated below:

A. A minimum of 12 semester hours in graduate-level reading courses with at least one course in 1 and 2 and in 3 or 4:

1. Foundations or survey of reading.
   The content of this basic course is related exclusively to reading instruction or the psychology of reading. Such a course ordinarily would be the first in a sequence of reading courses.

2. Diagnosis and correction of reading disabilities.
   The content of this course or these courses includes the following: causes of reading disabilities; observation and interview procedures; diagnostic instruments; standard and informal tests; report writing; materials and methods of instruction.

3. Clinical or laboratory practicum in reading.
   A clinical or laboratory experience might be an integral part of a course or courses in the diagnosis and correction of reading disabilities. Students diagnose and treat reading disability cases under supervision.

4. Supervision and curriculum in reading.
   This course involves the study of selected curriculum in reading; an understanding of the functions and duties of the reading supervisor or consultant and the effective ways of implementing them.

B. At least one graduate-level course in each of the following content areas:

1. Measurement and/or evaluation.
   This course includes one or more of the following studies: the principles and practices of test construction and the selecting, administering, scoring, and interpreting of group standardized tests; the nature, theory, function, and use of individual intelligence tests; the theory, function, and use of tests of personality.

2. Child and/or adolescent psychology or development.
   This course stresses how children and/or adolescents mature

[5]Prepared 1961 by the Committee on Professional Standards, International Reading Association. Now under revision.

and develop with emphasis on school activities and their relation to normal, healthy development.

3. Personality and/or mental hygiene.

   This course includes one or more of the following studies: the nature, development, and patterns of personality and the methods of the change; personality theories and their contributions to understanding the dynamics of personality; integration of psychological knowledge and principles and their relation to mental health; etiological factors, differential diagnosis, and methods used in the correction of behavior problems.

4. Educational psychology.

   This course includes one or both of the following studies: the study of behavior, development, school environment, conditions for learning, and methods of assessment; the theories of learning and their implications for classroom practices.

C. The remaining semester hours in reading and/or related areas—the following courses being recommended:

1. Literature for children and/or adolescents.

2. Organization and supervision of reading programs.

3. Research and the literature in reading.

4. Foundations of education.

5. Principles of guidance.

6. Nature of language.

7. Communications.

8. Speech and hearing.

9. Exceptional child.

10. Any additional courses listed under A and B.

FOR FURTHER READING

The Administrator and the School Reading Program. Proceedings of the Second Annual Hofstra University Reading Conference, Hempstead, N.Y., 1962. (Can be ordered directly from the Hofstra Reading Center. $1.50.)

NEWTON, J. ROY. *Reading in Your School*. New York: McGraw-Hill, 1960. Chap. 11, "The Administrator's Role in Reading."

STRANG, RUTH, and LINDQUIST, DONALD M. *The Administrator and the Improvement of Reading*. New York: Appleton-Century-Crofts, 1960.

STRANG, RUTH; MCCULLOUGH, CONSTANCE M.; and TRAXLER, ARTHUR E. *The Improvement of Reading*. 3d ed. New York: McGraw-Hill, 1961. Pp. 76–79.

UMANS, SHELLEY. "The Responsibility of the Reading Consultant," *Reading Teacher*, XVII (September 1963), 17–20.

CHAPTER 3

RELATIONSHIPS WITH TEACHERS

The reading consultant's major task is to work with teachers to improve reading instruction in the classroom, and to this end the consultant should make it apparent, especially to new teachers, that he does provide service to the teacher. The areas of service include (1) evaluation, (2) classroom organization, (3) provision of materials, (4) observations and interclass visitations, (5) demonstrations, (6) encouraging teachers to participate in research, and (7) leadership on a reading committee.

Evaluation

THE SELECTION OF TESTS. Often the reading consultant will be asked to help in selecting tests for a schoolwide testing program. Working carefully with department heads, supervisors, and teachers, he should be able to influence the adoption of reliable and valid tests especially suited to the needs of the school or school system. *that meet the objectives*

PROPER USE OF TESTS. After the tests are selected, the reading consultant can promote their most effective use by encouraging teachers to study the accompanying manuals as carefully as possible; usually he will conduct a workshop to familiarize teachers with the manuals. Whatever his means of communication, he should stress at least three considerations in conducting tests. First, he must make sure that the teachers know clearly *how to administer and score the tests*. A straight, thoroughgoing reading of the instruction manual should solve this problem of mechanics. Second, he should inform the teacher on *how to interpret the results of the testing*—that is, how to make an interpretation that tells the teacher how his students fare in relation to other students on their grade level and in their school or school system. Many considerations are involved in arriving at a valid interpretation: (1) The teacher should be urged to consider the mean intelligence of the school population. For instance, if the students' average intelligence quotient is high—say, 115—then a test result showing them to be about one year above the national norm stated in the manual should not be considered particularly unusual. (2) The teacher should be advised to view the test results only as a rough measurement, especially when he is just beginning to compare students in the classroom. (3) In making decisions about reading levels, the teacher should be urged not to consider one test score, one standardized measurement, as all-important, but to take into account other forms of appraisal as well. (4) The teacher should be encouraged to consider all the possible meanings of a test score. He should understand that a low vocabulary score may indicate a word recognition problem rather than a word meaning problem. He should recognize that high scores in arithmetic computation coupled with low scores in reading comprehension or vocabulary may indicate a disability in reading. And he should understand that any score, high or low, gives only a rough indication of reading level and does not pinpoint strengths or weaknesses in particular areas of reading. — need to analyze all of the items.

TIPS

TEST ADMINISTRATION

1. Teachers administering an unfamiliar test should take it themselves before giving it to students.
2. Teachers should prepare for the administration of a standardized test just as they would a lesson.
3. Directions must be given exactly as printed, or the results of the testing may be invalid.
4. If teachers must hand-score the tests, the consultant should offer his assistance.

The third consideration to be stressed by the reading consultant involves the purpose of testing; the consultant should help teachers to understand *how to use the results of a testing program.* He should point out the values and limitations of testing as an aid to classroom organization (see pp. 64–65, 68–69). He should emphasize the use of tests as indicators of the need for further diagnosis. And he should show teachers how test results may signal a need to alter instructional methods or materials.

MAINTAINING DAY-TO-DAY EVALUATIONS. The reading consultant can help the teacher to advance from a mere initial study of test results toward a day-to-day examination of the weaknesses and strengths of individual learners in the classroom. The consultant can help the teacher to understand how to use diagnostic tools as part of his daily teaching so that over a period of time the teacher can develop an accurate picture of the reading progress of individual students. Several standardized tests and informal measures of evaluation that the teacher will find eminently useful are discussed in the chapter on "Evaluation," pp. 64–75.

To be useful, however, the results of this periodic evaluation of individual students must be entered in records to which the teacher may constantly refer. The consultant can be of great service to a teacher by helping to devise an effective record-keeping technique that saves time. One method is to maintain a system of file cards or folders containing statistical and discursive information about each student. Skill checklists are also valuable (see pp. 78–80). The folder shown on pages 29–32 is an example of a printed folder devised by one reading specialist.

USING THE RESULTS OF DAY-TO-DAY EVALUATION. The reading consultant should help the teacher to make use of the evaluations of the reading progress of individual students. First, the consultant can show that accurate evaluation gives the teacher an intelligent basis for referring severely retarded readers to the consultant for further diagnosis or to a reading teacher for remedial help. If a student requires the aid of a reading teacher, the consultant can help coordinate the efforts of the reading teacher and the classroom teacher so that learning is reinforced rather than divided. If no special reading teacher is available, the consultant can help the classroom teacher with the retarded readers. Second, the consultant can show that accurate evaluation permits the teacher to direct instruction toward individual needs. Organizing an effective program to care for individual needs is an important part of the consultant's services to the teacher.

Classroom Organization

The reading consultant can help the teacher to develop patterns of organization that will provide most effectively for individual differences. Such classroom organization will provide for several types of grouping, depending on need and purpose. Flexibility should be the all-important concept in organizational plans.

THE WHOLE CLASS AS A GROUP. Addressing the entire class as a single group may be occasioned (1) when introducing a new unit or a new topic (special assignments and individualized directions, of course, would be the follow-up to this introduction); (2) when reviewing certain concepts in areas where all or nearly all the students have shown a deficiency in the application of a skill; and (3) when concluding or summarizing a unit or topic. In this last instance, even though small groups or individuals may have worked on separate parts of the topic or unit, the whole group together may benefit by a bringing together of all the knowledge and skills individually acquired.

READING-LEVEL GROUPS. To divide the entire class into three or more groups according to approximate reading levels allows the use of basal readers at levels of difficulty closest to each child's achievement level.

INTEREST AND RESEARCH GROUPS. Although students usually chum together or develop informal groups because of common interests or problems rather than because of any similarity of reading levels, the teacher can often take advantage of these informal groupings to get students collectively interested in some instruction in the reading program.

READING-NEEDS GROUPS. Although the grouping of students according to reading level may be the more or less permanent arrangement in class, the teacher on occasion may wish to draw from these various levels certain students who share a common reading problem and form them into a temporary "need group." For instance, although John may be in the top reading-level group, Teresa and Bob in the middle group, and Jack and Grace in the lower group, they may all have a problem in pronouncing a phonic element or in finding the main idea in a paragraph. Joining these children from the various reading-level groups permits the teacher to concentrate on such a problem.

An occasional grouping of students according to need is a valuable device no matter whether the teacher has arranged his class according to reading levels or whether he normally works with individuals or teams of students. Under either arrangement, need grouping offers both economy and flexibility in teaching.

INDIVIDUALIZATION. Some teachers are experimenting with an individualized reading approach, which replaces the reading-level grouping and the step-by-step basal reader method. In this approach a variety of books are used and students are permitted—with guidance—to select their own books. The teacher then meets with each student individually to help him with reading problems and to guide him through the developmental program. Such a procedure may usefully employ the reading-needs grouping.

TEAMS. In the team approach the class is broken down into groups of two or more students working together. The plan usually takes one of two forms: (1) In *team learning,* the students on each team work together and help one another in learning new concepts, in applying skills, and in reviewing. With guidance from the teacher, they seek their own methods of learning, using materials provided by the teacher. (2) In *tutoring,* one student is appointed teacher of a specific skill and works with one or more other students in need of help. An organizational plan like this naturally demands detailed preparation by the student and the teacher.

INDEPENDENT ACTIVITIES. Finally, the reading consultant can help the classroom teacher by suggesting independent activities in which other students can be engaged while the teacher is directly helping one particular individual or group. In the Resources section, pp. 84–96, will be found a list of suggested activities together with some sources of further information.

WORK BOOKS

Name of Reading Workbook	Date Begun	Date Completed

WORD PERCEPTION INSTRUCTION

Skills	Date Begun	Date Completed
Consonants		
Consonant Digraphs		
Blends		
Vowels (Short)		
Vowels (Long)		
Vowel Digraphs		
Syllabication		
Accented Syllables		
Dictionary		
Diacritical Marks		
Simple Affixes		
Higher Lev. Affixes		
Word Analysis Workbooks		
Basic Word Lists		

Spelling

BOOKS READ-INSTRUCTIONAL

Name of Book	Gr. Level	Date Begun	Date Completed

Compiled by Sr. M. Julitta, O.S.F.
The Cardinal Stritch College, Milwaukee, Wis.
First Form, 1946; Revisions: 1953, 1961
May not be reprinted without permission

Reprinted with the permission of Cardinal Stritch College and Sr. M. Julitta, O.S.F.

SUMMARY OF DIAGNOSIS:

Type of Difficulty:

Probable Causes:

Recommendations:

TESTS ADMINISTERED DURING ATTENDANCE

Date	INTELLIGENCE	Form	Exam.	C.A.	M.A.	I.Q.	% ile Norm.
	ACHIEVEMENT	Form	Subject	Grade Equiv.	Age Equiv.	% ile Norm.	Gain

TOTAL GAIN IN READING:

Name of Test	Years	Months
	Gains	

Total Gains in Reading Level: From _____ to _____ grade level.

Levels at Dismissal: Instructional Reading _____ Independent Reading _____

ORAL DIAGNOSTIC RECORD

Fixations per 100 Words _____ Regressions per 100 Words _____ Rate per Minute _____

Remarks:

TELEBINOCULAR VISUAL SCREENING _____

AUDIOMETER: Right Ear _____
                     Left Ear _____

CONFERENCES — PARENTS, SCHOOLS, AGENCIES

ADDITIONAL OBSERVATIONS AND REMARKS

FINAL RESULTS

RECOMMENDATIONS:

Name................................ (Surname) .... (First) .... (Middle) .... Birthday.......... (Yr.) .... (Mo.) ...... (Day) ...... Age.......... (Years) .... (Months) ...... Grade..........

Address................................ (Street) .... (City) .... (Zone) .... (State) .... Telephone.......... Father's Name.......... Mother's Name..........

School................................ Address.......... (Street) .... (City) .... (Zone) .... (State) .... Telephone.......... Teacher..........

Referred to Clinic by.......... Date.......... Reasons for Referral..........

Change in Address.......... Telephone.......... School..........

TEST RECORD — SCHOOL HISTORY

Date	INTELLIGENCE					ACHIEVEMENT				
	Form	C.A.	M.A.	I.Q.	%ile Norm.	Form	Subject	Grade Equivalent	Age Equivalent	%ile Norm.

PRELIMINARY TESTS ADMINISTERED AT CLINIC

Date	INTELLIGENCE						READING CAPACITY		ACHIEVEMENT	
	Form	Exam.	C.A.	M.A.	I.Q.	%ile Norm.	Form	Subject	Grade Equiv.	Age Equiv.	%ile Norm.

DURRELL DIAGNOSTIC Date..........
Administrator:

	Grade Equiv-alent		DIAGNOSTIC TESTS Date..........		
1. Oral Reading (Speed)		Skill	Administrator:	Source	Grade Equiv. alent
2. Oral Reading (Comprehension)					
3. Silent Reading (Speed)					
4. Silent Reading (Comprehension)					
5. Listening Comprehension					
6. Word Flash					
7. Word Analysis					
8. Spelling					

INFORMAL RDG. OBSERVATIONS:

Date	Instructional Level	Independent Level	Hearing Comp.

Remarks:

ADDITIONAL PRELIMINARY INFORMATION

Level of Rdg. Materials in School:

Type of Rdg. Instruction:

BOOKS READ — INDEPENDENT

Name of Book	Gr. Level	Com-pleted	Name of Book	Gr. Level	Com-pleted	Name of Book	Gr. Level	Com-pleted	Name of Book	Gr. Level	Com-pleted

Materials

INSTRUCTIONAL MATERIALS. In performing the important task of helping teachers to select textbooks and supplementary reading materials, the reading consultant should, if possible, set up a display or center where teachers may look over samples of materials. Whatever his means of offering suggestions, however, the consultant should make sure that three types of material are included in the review: (1) instructional materials to meet a specific need, (2) practice materials published for the improvement of specific reading skills, and (3) either procedure outlines or specific materials designed by the consultant to meet particular needs, such as outlining and notetaking. In addition, the reading consultant should strive to introduce multilevel materials into the classroom, especially for content-area teachers, and he should help teachers to establish classroom libraries.

PROFESSIONAL INFORMATION. The reading consultant should provide himself and teachers with a variety of written materials—those of his own devising as well as published materials. These should offer information on which sound decisions can be based in selecting instructional materials and tests, charting a student's course of study, and developing a good reading program in general.

First, there is the information used to evaluate individual items or factors: (1) data evaluating the strengths and weaknesses of specific tests;[6] (2) data evaluating the strengths and weaknesses of any of the basal reading series; (3) information gained from parents (possibly through questionnaires) regarding a child's reading readiness; and (4) information about the readability of certain trade books or instructional materials. This readability information can take the form of annotated bibliographies compiled by the consultant, commercial bibliographies in print, special analyses prepared at the request of a teacher, or a general file of analyses available to all teachers seeking references or guidance.

Second, there is the information describing research currently in progress or presenting the statements and opinions of authorities on various areas of reading. Among the topics of interest might be (1) the relation between the phonics taught in reading and success in spelling; (2) the results of individualized reading programs; (3) the effects of delaying instruction in reading; (4) the effects of beginning reading instruction in kindergarten; (5) the effects of an overemphasis on one word-attack skill, such as phonics; (6) the value in teaching SQ3R (the study formula introduced by Francis Robinson in *Effective Study*); (7) the relation of reading instruction in the content areas to success in the content areas; and (8) the new trends in reading instruction (such as programed instruction, the Initial Teaching Alphabet

[6]See pp. 68–69 in the chapter on "Evaluation."

system, the linguistics approach). Most important, the reading consultant should keep teachers posted on information he has gathered at reading conferences and on information he has drawn from his own reading.

Third, there is the information contained in brochures, summaries, and printed reviews describing recent publications or various developments in reading. Such material is usually available in quantity from publishers.

Finally, there are the books, periodicals, and other resource materials which the reading consultant keeps in his professional library. This library should be kept up to date; it should contain not only a collection of basic works (see the Resources section for lists of professional books, pamphlets, and periodicals) but also any new publications of major importance. It is equally important that the consultant devise a suitable arrangement for organizing or cataloging this material so that he knows what is available and where he can readily find desired information for himself or for teachers with whom he wishes to share his library materials.

Observations and Interclass Visitations

CONSULTANT'S OBSERVATIONS. When a consultant sits in on a class in progress and observes student and teacher performance, it is ordinarily *not* for the purpose of making evaluations for the administrator. Even though the consultant cannot avoid discussing classroom situations with supervisors or department heads, he visits a classroom chiefly to help the *teacher*.

Both the consultant and the classroom teachers should know the school's policy regarding the consultant's observations—that is, whether there will be unscheduled as well as scheduled observations and whether the consultant, when asked by a teacher to observe, may feel free to pop in during his free moments without warning the teacher in advance. It should be understood, however, that *unscheduled observations* are not entirely suitable for getting thorough information—chiefly because their duration is usually too brief. They are valuable only if the consultant wishes to see a teacher about a specific problem, if he desires to gather, rather informally, certain information relative to reading in the classroom, or if he feels that an unscheduled observation can be a worthwhile prelude to a planned observation.

Planned observations occur during a specified time agreed upon in advance by the teacher and the consultant. The consultant's purpose in making these planned observations is (1) to acquire an overview of the total program in the school, (2) to meet the request of a teacher, (3) to see a technique the teacher is using, or (4) to observe specific students. Before going to the class, the consultant should certainly have a firm idea of what he is looking for. After the observation he should arrange a conference with the teacher as soon as possible, preferably the same day; and in the weeks that follow he should evaluate how the teacher follows through on suggestions.

TIPS

CONSULTANT'S OBSERVATIONS

1. The reading consultant's role is different from that of a supervisor. He should try to keep the observation as informal as possible. He should not give the teacher a list of things he is going to look for, because the teacher may then create a teaching situation to fit the expectations of the consultant and not conduct the class in his usual manner.

2. Ordinarily the consultant should not take notes during the observation. The consultant's purpose is to *help* the teacher, and few teachers can be helped who are made to feel that in the room there is a supervisor intent upon criticizing and writing down critical notes. (Of course, some teachers may not be bothered by notetaking, and in these cases the consultant should feel free to take notes.)

3. In the conferences held after the observation, the consultant should begin by mentioning a number of positive points to the teacher. Then he should choose one of the negative points and, with the teacher, work out a plan for remedying the problem.

TEACHER OBSERVATIONS. Teachers, as well as consultants, should be given the opportunity to observe classroom situations other than their own. If planned and executed properly, such observations can be a valuable learning process for the teacher. The consultant's task is to set up arrangements that do not involve a lot of red tape. A teacher's visit to other classrooms may be occasioned (1) when a consultant observes a particularly effective teaching method and wants a teacher to observe the method; (2) when a teacher has heard about a new or different method he wishes to observe; (3) when a teacher wishes to visit another school system to observe new techniques (for example, an ungraded class) or when the consultant wants a teacher to observe such techniques; and (4) when a consultant wishes a teacher to visit classrooms to look at bulletin boards and materials in use (short visits after school serve this purpose).

Demonstrations

From time to time the reading consultant will want to demonstrate to one or more teachers certain instructional techniques or the use of specific reading materials. The consultant may conduct a classroom session for an *individual teacher* when—in the course of a planned conference, observation, or informal chat—it is recognized that a teacher needs to improve some part of his instruction or needs help in the use of materials new to him.

However, a demonstration observed by an individual teacher may be occasioned simply when the consultant desires to try out a new method in the classroom, such as a new method for teaching vocabulary. This kind of observation takes on the nature of an experimentation.

Demonstrations by the consultant before a *group of teachers* may be prompted by the consultant's desire (1) to share new techniques with all teachers; (2) to demonstrate a technique in order to help overcome a specific weakness in the reading program; (3) to demonstrate the use of new material; or (4) to show content-area teachers how teaching reading skills can be incorporated into the teaching of content material.

TIPS

TEACHER OBSERVATIONS

1. The teacher observing another classroom should know precisely what to look for, and the teacher being observed should know why the observation is being made.

2. The teacher being observed should be a secure person, one not easily rattled.

3. No one teacher ought to be subjected to observation so often that other teachers begin to feel that he is being set up as the "perfect" teacher. Such constancy of attention can only stir up resentment against him.

Research

Another important relationship between the reading consultant and the teacher involves the conducting of research and experimentation in the school setting. This classroom experimentation can be one of the most effective ways in which the reading consultant can bring about changes in classroom activities, for a teacher actively involved in experimentation can persuade *himself* of the effectiveness of new methods suggested by the consultant. If he catches the spirit of shared research, the teacher alters his methods more willingly and, because of increased self-confidence, more effectively than he does if he is bluntly told to try a new method or if on his own initiative he hazards a new method he has read about in a journal.

Experimentation can take either of two forms—*action research* (informal experimentation) or *formal research* (involving controlled environments). The following are examples of these two approaches.

Action research
1. Some teachers decide to try to improve textbook reading in social

studies and to improve vocabulary by teaching new and important words and concepts prior to having their students read each new chapter.

2. The teachers agree to try the method in their classrooms, planning and evaluating together.

3. After a month's trial, they make decisions about the value of the method.

Formal research

1. Some teachers feel a need to improve the teaching of reading in social studies.

2. Through a careful survey of existing research in the field, they agree that the method of preteaching new and important concepts before students read a new chapter may be a useful technique.

3. They set up two experimental groups (to receive prevocabulary work) and two control groups (to receive no prevocabulary work). They try to control as many variables as possible—sex, teacher enthusiasm, intelligence, and so forth. They measure current reading ability, vocabulary development, and competence in social studies.

4. After a semester, tests of reading ability, vocabulary development, and social studies competence are given again as they were at the beginning of the semester. Conclusions and decisions about the value of the method are tentatively drawn after careful analysis.

The reading consultant, of course, should also disseminate and interpret pertinent findings from current research conducted outside the school or local school system. The classroom teacher, too, should be encouraged to contribute ideas derived from his reading of professional materials, ideas which the consultant may wish to pass along to other teachers.

TIPS

Research and Experimentation

1. If some aspect of instruction seems to be questionable (for example, if there is doubt about the teaching of oral reading, or if the staff is divided in regard to the emphasis placed on it in various grades), then a study of pertinent research findings may help to clarify ideas and stimulate thought.

2. In considering a revision of the reading program, the consultant and the classroom teachers should try to spot any research related to the evaluation of programs or research designs particularly suited to the school.

Reading Committee

In the school or school system the reading consultant should be a member of the reading committee whose purpose is to promote an ever progressing reading program. In addition to the consultant, the committee should be composed of a representative of the administration, a guidance counselor, and teachers representing both grade-level and subject-matter areas; other specialists, such as a nurse or a psychologist, might be drawn in as consultants. The major task of the committee should be to evaluate the reading program continually and to take necessary steps toward improving the program—with the consultant taking a leadership role in making and implementing decisions.[7]

For further reading

AUSTIN, MARY C.; BUSH, CLIFFORD L.; and HUEBNER, MILDRED H. *Reading Evaluation.* New York: Ronald Press, 1961.

HARRIS, ALBERT J. (ed.). *Readings on Reading Instruction.* New York: McKay, 1963. Chap. 5, "Measuring Reading Outcomes and Determining Needs"; Chap. 6, "Grouping for Effective Reading Instruction"; Chap. 7, "Individualized Reading"; Chap. 13, "Materials for the Reading Program."

NEWTON, J. ROY. *Reading in Your School.* New York: McGraw-Hill, 1960. Chap. 6, "Testing Programs"; pp. 131–42, "The Classroom Teacher and Reading."

SMITH, NILA BANTON. *Reading Instruction for Today's Children.* Englewood Cliffs, N.J.: Prentice-Hall, 1963. Chap. 5, "Approaches Differ"; Chap. 6, "Grouping Plans Take on New Forms"; Chap. 7, "Individualized Instruction Receives Attention."

TINKER, MILES A., and McCULLOUGH, CONSTANCE. *Teaching Elementary Reading.* 2d ed. New York: Appleton-Century-Crofts, 1962. Chap. 16, "Appraisal of Reading Growth"; Chap. 17, "The Organization and Administration of the Reading Program."

UMANS, SHELLEY. *New Trends in Reading Instruction.* New York: Bureau of Publications, Teachers College, Columbia Univ., 1963. Chap. 3, "Flexible Grouping in Reading Instruction."

---

[7]For further information on reading committees, consult the following works: J. Roy Newton, *Reading in Your School* (New York: McGraw-Hill, 1960), pp. 12–17; Elizabeth A. Simpson, *Helping High School Students Read Better* (Chicago: Science Research Associates, 1954), pp. 52–58.

CHAPTER 4

RELATIONSHIPS WITH OTHER MEMBERS OF THE SCHOOL STAFF

Although maintaining a positive and active relationship with administrators and classroom teachers is of great importance, the rapport that the reading consultant establishes with other members of the staff is also essential for the success of a reading program. This chapter is designed to explore some of the most important relationships—with curriculum and supervision specialists, with the psychologist, with the speech therapist or consultant, with the nurse, with guidance personnel, with the school librarian, and with the secretarial and custodial staff.

Relationships with Curriculum and Supervision Specialists

Under the general classification of curriculum and supervision specialists may be included (1) the *curriculum coordinator,* who is trained to plan, improve, and evaluate the school curriculum, (2) the *supervisor,* who is primarily concerned with the improvement and evaluation of instruction, (3) the *department heads,* who, in a departmental setup in a single school, are concerned with both curriculum development and instruction improvement in special content areas, and (4) the *content-area specialists,* who, in a school system, are similarly concerned with both curriculum development and instruction improvement in special content areas; these last are often called supervisors or coordinators of social studies, science, or one of the other disciplines. In some schools—dependent upon size, location, organization, or wealth of the community—these positions may be combined in a variety of ways. However, regardless of the titles given to the persons discharging these various responsibilities, the reading consultant should be aware of the several responsibilities and know for certain to whom they are delegated.

It is important for the consultant to consider both how the curriculum and supervision specialists can *give* aid to the reading program and how they can *receive* aid in performing duties related to the reading program. And in this regard it is important for the consultant to know the respective responsibilities and limits of the work of each staff member.

How the Consultant May Assist the Specialists. The reading consultant has several responsibilities that involve aiding the curriculum and supervision specialists in their activities. First, he should hold scheduled meetings with curriculum and supervision specialists in order to clarify the philosophy behind the reading program, to gain support for the reading program, or to pinpoint specific aspects of the reading program.

TIPS

Conducting Meetings with Specialists

1. Limit the scope of the meetings; attack a small but vital area.
2. Prior to the meeting, send an agenda to the specialists.
3. Stick to the agenda.
4. Don't dominate the meeting.
5. Serve refreshments.
6. Begin and end the meeting promptly.
7. Distribute a follow-up summary for participants and absentees.

Second, the reading consultant should assist curriculum and supervision specialists in evaluating existing curricula in relation to the instructional program in reading. The examples of this type of assistance vary widely in character. After observing various teaching situations, the consultant may suggest to specialists certain measures to overcome the failure of certain teachers to use multilevel materials to meet the individual needs of students. After conferring with the school librarian, the consultant may be able to suggest ways of improving the students' library skills through assignments or instruction in the classroom. The consultant and the content-area supervisors, too, can work together to help those students who, though able to read and retain details pertinent to main ideas, tend to be indiscriminate readers who accept what an author says without question.

Third, the reading consultant may aid specialists in setting up new curricula that give specific attention to the teaching of reading skills. He may prepare lists of developmental reading skills and suggest some sequence for introducing different skills. Or he may compile lists of reading skills pertinent to the content areas. Either list may bear on curriculum revision.

Fourth, the consultant may assist curriculum and supervision specialists in evaluating the reading program within a content area. In the light of this evaluation, all concerned can plan effective methods of improving the program. The preliminary discussions would center on methods and materials to promote the reading program at all grade levels and in all content areas.

For example, the consultant can demonstrate how a retarded reader, though using a book at his third-grade reading level, may still learn content at his fifth-grade level; or, on the other hand, the consultant may demonstrate how an accelerated student in grade 6 can study in depth by using books beyond his grade level. In any case, the consultant should encourage classroom organizations that provide a wide and wise selection of texts and materials on several levels.

Equally important, the consultant should follow through and find means of evaluating programs newly instituted. Perhaps the new programs may be the subject of controlled experiments. For example, half of the social studies teachers may be chosen to use SQ3R as a study skill, while the other half continue with the traditional method; later the results can be compared to determine what a permanent program should be. Or perhaps one group of reading teachers may be selected to use the individualized approach to reading while another group continues with traditional methods. Evaluations of such programs should embrace test results, teacher judgments, and records of supplementary reading, particularly the use of the library.

Fifth, the reading consultant may assist curriculum and supervision specialists in evaluating methods and materials being used in the total curriculum. In this respect, the consultant may—

Apply readability formulas in judging texts, so that the texts are appropriate to the reading levels of the students.

Provide book lists that measure books according to their readability, from "very easy" to "difficult," and thereby promote and guide suitable outside reading of students.

Develop, with the help of the staff, a set of criteria for selecting and evaluating materials (see the Resources section, p. 80).

Sixth, the reading consultant can assist supervisors and department heads in identifying and treating students with reading problems. He may—

Establish a referral system for students in need of special reading help.

Diagnose students referred to him by curriculum and supervision specialists.

Suggest how students needing help with their reading problems may obtain that help within the classroom, or perhaps volunteer to give this help himself.

Establish remedial programs for students with severe reading disabilities.

Suggest ways in which the supervisor or department head may induce the content-area teachers to complement the help being given in a remedial class.

How the Specialists May Assist the Consultant. Through active support and a positive attitude the curriculum and supervision specialists can give the reading consultant a great deal of assistance. First, they can make a continuous effort to understand and interpret the reading program at all grade levels and in all content areas. Second, the specialists—particularly the department heads and content-area specialists—can help to identify staff members who are enthusiastic about improving reading instruction and who may be especially effective in helping the consultant to initiate a new reading program or to improve an existing program.

Third, the curriculum and supervision specialists can smooth the way for the consultant to work with various staff members. They can arrange a coffee time that allows a friendly setting for meetings between the consultant and staff members. They can give permission to hold meetings on school time rather than after school. And they can make it possible, without red tape, for teachers to be relieved of classroom duties so that they may observe how reading skills are being taught in other classrooms.

Finally, the curriculum and supervision specialists can facilitate the work of the reading consultant by providing him with various mechanical aids. For example, they can arrange for the printing or duplicating of minutes of all meetings—the minutes to be distributed to those who attended the meetings as well as to those who were unable to attend.

Relationships with the Psychologist

If the school system employs a psychologist, the information he gathers may be crucially valuable to all personnel who work with students having a severe reading disability. It is the responsibility of both the psychologist and the reading consultant to evaluate and discuss such information with the student's teachers and with special service personnel—including, of course, the reading teacher.

In school systems having no staff psychologist, the reading consultant should have a list of public clinics, private doctors, or local universities to whom he can refer the severely retarded reader suffering from debilitating emotional problems.

How the Psychologist May Help the Reading Program. The psychologist's services may be valuable to the reading consultant in a number of ways. First, the psychologist may test students referred to him by the consultant in order to determine more exactly their mental capacities or to determine any emotional disability hampering their progress. Second, he may counsel those students who require this type of guidance. Third, he may refer to the proper persons those students who need extensive professional help. Fourth, he may confer with the consultant to determine the best method of working with a child having emotional problems. Such a conference might uncover to what extent a child's emotional problem influences his ability to benefit from instruction; it might determine what kind of teacher or what teaching method is most suitable for the child; it might disclose what kind of classroom atmosphere is most conducive to the child's progress (whether, for example, there should be increased or lessened pressure, or more or less responsibility); it may determine whether the child responds best to individual or to group instruction; or, finally, it could reveal the extent of the parents' role in the situation.

Fifth, the psychologist may confer with the consultant about experimentation with various methods of reading instruction. He might act as an adviser to the consultant who is setting up and evaluating experimental situations. Sixth, he may promote mental health practices in all classrooms by encouraging teachers to accept the wide range of differences among their students and by helping them to plan programs adjusted to this range. Finally, the psychologist can help to convince the administration of the need for remedial classes, flexible approaches, and other necessary adjustments to individual differences.

How the Consultant May Help the Psychologist. The reading consultant, in turn, has certain responsibilities toward the psychologist. He should maintain communication with the psychologist so that both of them are continually informed about the behavior and progress of students. Whenever a severe emotional disability seems to exist, the consultant should refer the retarded reader to the psychologist for a more intensive evaluation. Finally, he should participate with the psychologist in conferences with parents, administrators, and teachers.

Relationships with the Speech Specialist

The speech specialist is a staff member who can provide the consultant with valuable information about particular students. If the speech specialist is working with a student who is a retarded reader, the consultant and the speech specialist can confer to explore the possible relation between the student's speech and his reading difficulties and to make concrete plans complementing each other's work. If it is determined that the speech difficulties of the student are, in all probability, a significant factor in his reading disability, then the reading consultant and the speech specialist may agree that it is necessary to treat the speech disorder before remedial instruction in reading can be effective.

The speech specialist may also act as a consultant and help with developmental speech programs. In this case the reading consultant and speech consultant will want to synchronize such factors as scheduling, teaching conferences, observations, and class visits. The two consultants should iron out differences in philosophies when approaching such areas as phonics or phonetics, in-service programs, and remedial procedures.

Relationships with the School Nurse

The school nurse can contribute to the reading program by testing or screening the school population or selected students for visual, hearing, and other physical handicaps. Students who show disabilities should be referred by the nurse to the appropriate professional service for diagnosis and correction or treatment.

The reading consultant should make use of the student health records usually kept by the nurse, so that a history of illness, physical handicaps, extended absences for health reasons, or frequent visits to the nurse for real or imaginary illnesses may be taken into account in the diagnosis of reading disabilities. The consultant should cooperate with the nurse in constructing a referral list so that students may be directed to the proper person for visual and other medical diagnosis and treatment. Referrals should normally go through the nurse's office, especially if school policy prescribes that health referrals should follow this route. Nevertheless, the consultant's primary obligation is to be certain that the student receives the help he needs.

In schools that do not have nurses on their staff, the consultant should learn the location of health facilities such as public or university clinics or the names of vision and hearing specialists, so that outside referrals for testing or treatment may be made.

Relationships with Guidance Personnel

Since guidance personnel are in an especially advantageous position to assist the reading consultant, it is important that the consultant help them to view reading as part of each individual's total adjustment to school and to later life and to be aware of the close relation between reading problems and personality problems. With members of the guidance staff the reading consultant should form a relationship that encourages conferences about students with reading problems. Such a relationship will lead to close communication with the guidance department regarding such matters as testing programs, interviews with parents, and remedial programs.

Guidance counselors are also valuable allies in the total school reading program. They are concerned with the teaching of reading skills throughout the curriculum in order to strengthen the abilities of students in later employment and in college.

Guidance personnel can contribute to the reading program in a number of ways: (1) they can help obtain additional information about students, both by closely interpreting available data and by selecting appropriate tests; (2) they can assist in organizing in-service training programs that consider such topics as mental health, personality dynamics, counseling techniques, the effects of total environment on learning, and the use of standardized tests; (3) in the process of helping each student to clarify his educational and vocational goals, they can help him select books related to his interests; (4) they can help students to maintain good study habits; and (5) they can stress that extensive reading is important for college admission.

An example of how guidance personnel could help in a specific situation might here be useful. Perhaps the consultant wishes to set up interest groups featuring reading. Guidance personnel can draw on their knowledge of individual students in suggesting appropriate groups that would appeal to each student. Groups could be formed on the basis of vocational plans or interest in an occupation. Students could gather information by various means, including reading, and regularly report findings to one another.

Relationships with the School Librarian

Because the library stores a vast supply of books and other materials directed toward recreational and informational reading, it is of vital importance that the reading consultant and the librarian collaborate in building appropriate library skills and attitudes. In order to effect this collaboration, the consultant should follow these procedures: (1) He should acquaint the librarian in detail with the philosophy of the reading program, its purposes and goals. (2) He should discuss the wide range of reading interests and abilities the librarian may find within one class. If the ability range has been narrowed, or if there is some form of "track system" or schoolwide grouping, it is important that the librarian recognize the range of ability within each class. (3) He should acquaint the librarian with the specific reading problems of those students who have difficulty in selecting appropriate books. A plan should be worked out whereby the librarian can detect—perhaps from a symbol on the student's library card—what the student's independent reading level is. (4) He should solicit the aid of the librarian in selecting books for classroom libraries and in arranging for continuous circulation of books. (5) He should plan with the librarian the various grade levels at which specific library skills should be stressed. (6) He should help the librarian to select appropriate books on a wide variety of reading levels. (7) He should cooperate with the librarian in staging book fairs, exhibits, and book talks. (8) He should cooperate with the librarian in providing lists of books on a variety of topics. Special lists, for example, should be prepared for "Holiday Reading," "Summer Reading," and the like. (9) He should invite the librarian to visit classrooms in order to generate enthusiasm for reading, to describe new books, and so forth. (10) He should evaluate with the librarian the advantages and limitations of readability formulas.

Relationships with Nonprofessional Personnel

The reading consultant will find that members of the secretarial and custodial staffs can be invaluable in helping him to perform various tasks efficiently—but only if the reading consultant establishes rapport with these personnel and makes an effort to get them interested in the goals of the reading program. However, the consultant must recognize the everyday demands made upon these persons and not attempt to monopolize their services.

FOR FURTHER READING

NEWTON, J. ROY. *Reading in Your School*. New York: McGraw-Hill, 1960. Chap. 7, "The Staff and Reading"; Chap. 9, "School Psychologist and Special Services."

STRANG, RUTH; McCULLOUGH, CONSTANCE M.; and TRAXLER, ARTHUR E. *The Improvement of Reading*. 3d ed. New York: McGraw-Hill, 1961. Chap. 3, "Total Program for the Improvement of Reading."

CHAPTER **5**

IN-SERVICE TRAINING

Perhaps the most important group activity that the reading consultant will initiate and participate in is the in-service program in reading. A number of important principles should guide him as he prepares, conducts, and follows through with such programs.

In-service programs that reflect the realistic needs of the school and its staff have the best chance for success. By means of conferences with the consultant, questionnaires, and informal and formal group meetings, staff members should be given an opportunity to suggest the needs that they themselves have observed relative to reading instruction. But the reading consultant will no doubt discover needs overlooked by individual teachers, because he will have had the advantage of having made classroom observations, conducted demonstration lessons, synthesized the results of meetings with individuals and groups, analyzed questionnaires, and studied the results of standardized and informal tests. Analyzing all these activities together should make the consultant uniquely qualified to determine reading needs.

An in-service program that threatens the security of staff members cannot succeed. Nevertheless, if teachers are themselves to some degree dissatisfied with their classroom performance, they should be in a more receptive mood for the changes which in-service programs often presage. An in-service program stimulates an evaluation of the status quo, and reluctance or active resistance during the early stages of a program may be a healthy sign of the teachers' involvement rather than a sign of program failure.

The list that follows represents specific guides to conducting successful in-service programs.

1. The active support of teachers who are reputed to be extremely capable instructors and who are respected by other teachers greatly helps the reading consultant in organizing and conducting the in-service program.

2. Programs that try to accomplish too much in too short a time will not have lasting results.

3. Programs that require too much of the teachers' "free" time are likely to breed resentment and failure.

47

4. In-service reading programs that involve persons who teach in a subject area must reflect the goals and objectives of that area. To help ensure fuller cooperation from content-area teachers, the consultant should use the materials of their subject to demonstrate the application of specific reading skills.

5. To be successful, an in-service program must have the full support of the administration.

6. Participants in the in-service program should have the opportunity to share in both the planning and the evaluating of the program.

7. The consultant in charge of a systemwide program may be able to identify a need existing at all levels or a need existing at a particular grade level or in a particular subject field. Although meetings involving only grade or subject-area teachers may be important, programs organized around the entire staff of one institution will in all probability be most successful.

8. The reading consultant should capitalize on the interests and efforts of such groups as grade-level chairmen, guidance committees, and resource personnel.

TIPS

CONDUCTING IN-SERVICE PROGRAMS

1. Attractive conference rooms and refreshments are intangible aids during in-service sessions.

2. Written communications should be a follow-up to meetings and should be distributed to both participants and other staff members. It must be emphasized, however, that written communications at best merely supplement face-to-face oral communication.

Orientation

In some school systems orientation for new staff members begins in the spring when every new teacher slated to arrive the next fall is given a chance to visit the school and become acquainted with his future colleagues. Since not all of the new teachers will normally be free to visit on one appointed day, orientation must be kept informal. If time permits, the warm reception by the reading consultant may be followed by a tour of rooms, an introduction to other staff members, and the distribution of curriculum guides.

Many school systems hold formal orientation sessions in the fall before school officially opens. For new teachers the orientation program in reading must consider many skills and techniques already familiar to veteran teachers; hence *separate sessions* for new teachers should be scheduled when the topic is really of value to them alone. There are a number of topics that can profitably be discussed; those that follow would be of most interest to beginning teachers or to those new to the school.

1. The reading philosophy of the school system
2. The availability and use of curriculum guides
3. The materials available and the procedures for obtaining them[s]
4. The remedial program and how it relates to classroom teaching
5. Supplementary and recreational reading in the curriculum
6. The role of basal and co-basal readers in the total reading program
7. Library facilities (classroom, school, and community)
8. Reporting to parents
9. Testing programs
10. Cumulative records
11. Individualized reading programs[s]
12. New trends in reading instruction[s]

Joint meetings of new and veteran teachers should emphasize the reading consultant's services. The demonstration of a new practical instructional aid along with a display of new materials will help accomplish this aim. Every effort should be exerted to spark the enthusiasm of the group, since these first efforts may encourage interest later.

When School Starts

During the first few months of the school year the reading consultant will focus his attention on providing specific and definite services, particularly to new teachers. Especially during the first month of school the reading consultant should arrange his schedule in an attempt to visit each new teacher in the classroom. This visit should not be a formal observation but rather a casual visit to give on-the-spot assistance if possible or to make more definite arrangements for a return visit for a conference or observation. Such problems as grouping for instruction, arranging rooms, obtaining materials, and adapting the textbook or workbook to individual needs will be of concern to the new teacher.

Sometime during the first month of school, the reading consultant should assist with the analysis of student records, the study of cumulative records, and the interpreting of test results. Upon request the consultant should offer to demonstrate specific instructional methods.

[s]These topics should be of concern to veteran teachers as well.

As the Year Progresses

The reading consultant in various ways can serve all teachers and help them contribute to the total school program. In the pages that follow, these services are described in detail.

WORKSHOPS. A common need involving a number of teachers may warrant holding a workshop. A reading workshop, which should focus on a specific need area and emphasize practical helps in teaching, may take from a few hours to a few days, depending on the scope. Possible topics are "The Setting of Purposes in Reading," "Reading Skills in Science," "Word Analysis Program," and "Developing Critical Readers."

TIPS

CONDUCTING A WORKSHOP FOR TEACHERS

1. Give credit to individuals contributing to the workshop.
2. Secure for the teachers released time from regular school duties or schedule the meetings when groups of teachers are free (as in a departmentalized situation).
3. Begin and end sessions promptly.
4. Deal with a specific problem or area.
5. Organize a program with teacher participation rather than present a formal lecture.
6. Let attendance be voluntary.
7. Provide refreshments when possible.
8. Relate techniques to everyday teaching by using regular school materials.
9. Follow up the workshop sessions by distributing a brief summary of the proceedings.
10. Incorporate audio-visual techniques at every opportunity.
11. Provide for teacher evaluation of the sessions and incorporate their suggestions into the planning of future workshops.
12. Be realistic in recognizing school problems.

DEMONSTRATIONS. Demonstrations—given in response to a professed need on the part of one or more classroom teachers—are performed by the reading consultant, a teacher, or a university instructor and are witnessed by an individual teacher in his own classroom or by a group of teachers. The outline that follows, illustrating the procedure for teaching a phonic element, is an example of the kind of demonstration that will be effective in helping classroom teachers become better teachers of reading.

Perhaps some primary pupils have exhibited a need for help with the *tr* blend; in their reading they are missing or confusing such words as *tractor, trench,* and *treat.* A *tr* group is organized in order to help them learn the sound so that they may more easily attack such words in their reading. (The presentation here would be suitable in a basal or individualized plan.)

Auditory Discrimination

1. The teacher says, "Listen as I say these words: *tree, train, try.*" (The beginning sound should be emphasized but not distorted.)

2. "Can anyone tell me how these words are alike?" (The answer to be elicited is that they all sound alike at the beginning.)

Visual Discrimination

1. On the board or on a chart the teacher places the words *tree, train, try.*

2. A student is asked to go to the board and box in the parts that sound alike. (It should be elicited that all begin alike.)

Auditory Review

"Listen as I say these words and see if you can hear a word that begins with the sound in *tree* and *train.*" The teacher pronounces words like *trick, trap, house,* and *tall.* (For auditory review, groups of words should be few in number; each student should be given a chance to identify in a new group of words those words beginning with *tr.*)

Visual Review

1. The teacher places some words on the board or on a chart:

track	truck	dog
trip	house	treat
tick	tree	treasure

2. The teacher says, "Can anyone see the words that do not belong?" or "Come up and circle the words that begin with our sound." (Again, each student is given a chance.)

Blending

1. Using a known sight word, the teacher writes the word *him* on the board.

2. The teacher then erases the initial consonant sound, *h,* and substitutes the *tr* blend, forming *trim.*

3. He then pronounces the new word. This word should be an unfamiliar word that the students have not attacked (or have attacked inaccurately).

4. Following the same procedure with other pairs of words (such as *pray-tray, face-trace, blue-true*), the teacher asks the students to make the substitutions. (Again, each student should get a turn.)

Contextual Application

Each student should get a turn to read more difficult *tr* words in context. For example:

Will you (*try tramp treat*) me to a soda?

He pulled the [trigger] of his gun.

John and Jack like to jump on the tr[ampoline].

Further Follow-up Activities[9]

1. From magazines the teacher can clip pictures of objects whose names begin with the *tr* blend; these can be mounted in individual booklets or on a large class chart.

2. Exercises from phonic books or teacher-made materials can be completed as practice activities.

3. The teacher can use games that utilize the *tr* blend—games such as "Take" or "Word Wheels."

4. The teacher can use experience charts or stories in which *tr* words appear frequently.

Oral Reading

To be sure the instruction is applied and retained, the teacher should at some point give the students a purposeful opportunity to read orally material containing *tr* words. (*perhaps specially made material*)

BULLETINS. Printed material is an important form of communication between the reading consultant and teachers. The value of the information given will be lessened, however, if too many bulletins are distributed or if they tend to supplant the important group meetings or informal discussions.

Bulletins may report on the results of recent research and experiments in the system or may announce forthcoming events. The following example could be a part of a bulletin serving as a follow-up to a demonstration of a directed reading lesson.

---

[9]See the Resources section for other "Independent Activities."

A DIRECTED READING LESSON

Readiness (For this part of the lesson, no books are in the hands of students.)

A. The teacher first links the experience of the students to the material about to be read.

B. The teacher then attempts to motivate the students (capturing as much interest as possible and involving the students in the discussion).

C. He states the major purpose(s) of reading.

D. In discussing new words and concepts, the teacher—

1. Draws definitions and synonyms from students through discussion and questions.

2. Uses pictures when applicable.

3. Uses flash cards at times.

4. Provides the students with sentences with blanks to be filled in.

5. Writes on the board key sentences or phrases from the story.

6. Uses the glossary or dictionary (but avoids making this time a period for vocabulary study).

7. Uses charts.

Directed Reading (Books are distributed if directed reading is done in class, or reading may be assigned for homework.)

A. The students read silently in terms of the major purpose(s) determined under "Readiness."

B. The students may also read for secondary purposes, dependent upon level, group, or material.

C. The students should be guided toward full understanding of the material, in addition to fulfilling the purpose(s).

Check on Understanding

A. Checks on understanding may be written or oral or both.

B. Checks should include an appraisal of literal comprehension, interpretive ability, and vocabulary.

Skill Development

A. At this point a specific reading skill may be taught—preferably one growing from a need based on the reading.

B. Word analysis skills (as suggested in the phonics demonstration), a comprehension skill, a reference skill, or some other skill may be developed.

Rereading

A. Rereading may have taken place earlier during the check on understanding.

B. Some rereading for specific reasons related to content or skill development lesson may be performed.

Follow-up and Application

Enrichment or Additional Activities

TIPS

DISTRIBUTING BULLETINS

1. Don't send too many bulletins.
2. Limit the scope of the information covered.
3. Keep to one page if possible.
4. Make certain that bulletins summarizing meetings or demonstrations are distributed promptly—ideally the next day, certainly the next week.
5. Whenever possible, avoid generalities and give examples.
6. Give credit to individuals when credit is warranted.
7. Proofread! A misspelled word can distract from the information being offered.
8. Use a catchy title.
9. Have a generous supply of white showing on all four borders. Format is important.
10. For emphasis, use diagrams or cartoons.
11. If possible, vary the color of the ink.

CONFERENCES. In setting up a new in-service program or revising an existing one, the reading consultant should confer with the administrator. Conferences may also be held with the psychologist, the nurse, the social worker, or another staff member when it seems desirable to learn more about each other's roles and to plan an improvement of joint services.

The reading consultant will confer with teachers regarding demonstrations, course work, and workshop activities. Very important is the conference preceding and following the consultant's observation of a lesson—that is, a lesson given by the teacher—or a demonstration given by the consultant and witnessed by the teacher. The primary functions of the teacher-consultant conference are to maintain rapport with the teaching staff, to use every opportunity to discover needs, and to offer suggestions for improvement.

OBSERVATIONS AND INTERCLASS VISITATIONS. The in-service program should provide opportunities for teachers to observe others at work. Such observations and visitations should be aimed at a particular problem—for example, grouping students within the room for instruction, determining effective methods for improving oral reading, presenting phonic elements, or reading for the main idea. The reading consultant should consult the administrator in making necessary arrangements to free the teacher from his regular assignment long enough to make the observation or visit. The teacher to be observed should be consulted beforehand. It is important to follow up the conference to determine the benefits of the observation and to assist with the application of the techniques recommended.

COURSE WORK. Formal courses in reading instruction, with or without some type of credit, may be offered within a district. This kind of in-service training, although broad and structured, is another way of teaching teachers. Closed-circuit television offers many teachers front seats at demonstration lessons; some programs related to reading may be found on educational, or even commercial, television.

RESEARCH AND EXPERIMENTATION. No in-service program can be complete without making use of research and experimentation. Perhaps experimentation within the school can be conducted only on a modest scale and without the refinements of sophisticated research, but its value in stimulating teachers and introducing new ideas cannot be overestimated. Reports of these activities can be made by the reading consultant, individual teachers, or a department head and may be both written and oral. Some examples of possible experimentation are (1) looking into the relation between reading readiness scores and later success in reading; (2) placing library books in the classroom and keeping records of their use there as compared with their normal use in the school library; and (3) selecting, after the sixth week of school, those first-grade pupils in need of a more intensive reading readiness program and reassigning them to one room for reading instruction—the purpose being to determine whether in the long run this type of homogeneous grouping results in better readers.

Evaluation—both by stages and upon completion of an experiment—is the keynote of research. However, the stimulation and learning which teachers will experience are more important than strict scientific controls, when one considers this type of *informal experimentation* as an in-service tool.

Establishing a Professional Library

Providing a collection of professional publications and books to be available to teachers is an important kind of in-service training. Copies of journals and texts should be located in a central place and available for systematic circulation. If a budget for a professional library is not available, other steps should be taken early to begin building the professional library—possibly through gifts or loans from staff members.

If the school or school system lacks professional library facilities where volumes concerned with reading may be collected, perhaps a part of the student library might be used. Other possible locations exist, such as the reading consultant's office, the administrator's office, or the teachers' lounge. A professional library should be attractive and well organized according to a functional record-keeping system.

If teachers do not get to the professional library, the reading consultant should take it to them. Confronted by a specific and immediate problem in their classrooms, many teachers will read a pertinent article or section of a book suggesting solutions. This is an opportune time for the reading consultant to find specifically relevant material that will extend and enrich the teacher's efforts.

A list of suggested titles in reading for a professional library is presented in the Resources section, pp. 97–100.

FOR FURTHER READING

"Administrative Responsibilities for Providing In-service Training to Develop Sequential Learning," in *Sequential Development of Reading Abilities,* ed. Helen M. Robinson. (Supplementary Educational Monographs, No. 90.) Chicago: Univ. of Chicago Press, 1960. Pp. 180–201.

KOTTMEYER, W. "In-service Teacher Education in Reading," *International Reading Association Conference Proceedings,* VI (1961), 275–78.

MORRISON, C. "The Pre-service and In-service Education of Teachers of Reading," *International Reading Association Conference Proceedings,* VII (1962), 109–11.

National Society for the Study of Education. *In-service Education for Teachers, Supervisors, and Administrators.* (56th Yearbook, Part I.) Chicago: Univ. of Chicago Press, 1957.

CHAPTER 6

REMEDIAL READING

A strong reading program provides for all students. It includes developmental reading on all levels, corrective measures in the regular class situation, and remedial help for the seriously retarded readers.

In schools operating a remedial program, the reading consultant is usually responsible for the direction of this program. He is often responsible both for the coordination of the work of special reading teachers and for corrective or remedial work conducted by classroom teachers. In a number of school systems the reading consultant himself will be responsible for teaching severely retarded readers.

Definition of the Retarded Reader

Retarded readers are those students who are reading significantly below their capacity rather than merely below their grade level. Both factors—intellectual capacity and grade level—must be taken into consideration when defining a retarded reader. It is important that the reading consultant make such a definition clear to all school personnel, so that the remedial program does not become merely a convenient place to put students who have primarily emotional or disciplinary difficulties or severely limited intellectual capacities.

The consultant should also clarify the concept that a student may not always be retarded in all areas of reading but may often need special help with one or more specific skills. For example, a student can be particularly weak in the use of certain comprehension skills but strong in word analysis and adequate in vocabulary development.

Identification of the Retarded Reader

Identification and diagnosis of retardation in reading are complex and often misunderstood concepts. Identification precedes diagnosis. It is not concerned with the exact nature and causation of the problem; it merely indicates the presence of a difficulty. The process of identification includes the steps of screening and selecting.

The retarded reader is identified through the use of standardized tests, informal techniques, and teacher observation. Most often identification is made through a comparison of reading achievement and capacity. A number of schools will not accept for remedial instruction any students with below-average intelligence, but setting such an arbitrary level has inherent dangers: (1) many group intelligence tests used in school require that the student have an ability to read, so that a poor score may be a measure of poor reading rather than of low intelligence; (2) "slow learners" or "dull normal" students who read below their potential may actually be capable of substantial growth with special remedial attention.

The reading consultant must determine the number of students who can be helped effectively in the remedial situation and must also determine the level at which selection will begin. Priority should be given to the students with the greatest capacity for growth.

Although there is not always a clear relation between the scores that a student obtains on a standardized reading achievement test and the scores he achieves on an intelligence test, there is a positive relation between intellectual capacity and reading achievement. Hence, as a means of identifying retarded readers from among comparatively large groups, reading grade expectancy (that level at which a student should be able to read in the light of his potential) appears to be a valid criterion.

In the majority of school situations, the number of students who can be given special reading help is limited. Therefore it seems to make sense to select those who—on the basis of measured intellectual capacity—show the greatest potential for improvement. At the same time, it would be unrealistic to expect significant improvement for a youngster who—on the basis of reading grade expectancy—appears to be working up to his potential. In addition, a student may be a retarded reader but not a remedial "case." For instance, a beginning seventh-grader with an IQ of 130 and a reading grade of 7.0 is retarded in reading on the basis of capacity, but probably would not be selected for a remedial reading class.

According to Albert J. Harris, "A safe rule to follow is to select cases for remedial teaching in which reading is *at least* a year below the grade norm, and the difference between reading age and mental age is at least six months for children in the first three grades, nine months for children in grades four and five, or a year for children above the fifth grade."[10] George D. Spache points out some of the problems involved when using reading achievement tests in juxtaposition with intelligence tests and says that the "measurement of reading capacity through auditory comprehension," although still in its

---

[10]Albert J. Harris, *How to Increase Reading Ability* (4th ed.; New York: Longmans, Green, 1961), p. 299.

infancy, "holds distinct promise of contributing to improved prediction of reading capacity."[11]

There is no rule of thumb regarding when to begin remedial reading. This will vary with the particular school situation. Remediation is often started at the beginning of the third grade; if facilities are available, however, children in grade 2 may profit from early remediation. Most important is that the student's weaknesses be noted early. Early discovery followed by correction can prevent the mushrooming of problems and prevent severe disability.

Diagnosis of the Retarded Reader

The reading consultant will either direct the diagnosis of students identified as retarded readers or diagnose these students himself. The tools of diagnosis may include further tests of capacity (such as individual intelligence tests and listening tests) or additional tests of achievement. Following the administration of such tests, the diagnostician will rely on a number of techniques to pinpoint specific areas of need. The following is a partial list of *diagnostic tools.*

1. Standardized diagnostic tests for the purpose of locating specific weaknesses in reading.

2. Informal reading inventories to establish independent, instructional, and frustration reading levels as well as to pinpoint specific needs in reading.

3. Other informal tests focused on specific need areas: sight word tests; oral reading from textbooks; teacher-made comprehension skill tests.

4. School records: anecdotal files on an individual student; records of conferences with parents, teachers, and others; records of interviews with the student.

5. A recent report of a general physical examination (if one is not available, a physical examination should be given). Special emphasis should be placed on visual and auditory perception; the nurse, remedial reading teacher, or consultant may administer a visual screening test and an audiometer test. (See Chap. 7, p. 67, for a brief discussion of such tests.)

[11]George D. Spache, "Estimating Reading Capacity," in Helen M. Robinson (ed.), *Evaluation of Reading* (Chicago: Univ. of Chicago Press, 1958), p. 19. The following works are recommended for studies of reading grade expectancy: Guy L. Bond and Miles A. Tinker, *Reading Difficulties: Their Diagnosis and Correction* (New York: Appleton-Century-Crofts, 1957), pp. 76–81. Albert J. Harris, *How to Increase Reading Ability* (4th ed.; New York: Longmans, Green, 1961), pp. 299–302. Alice Horn, *The Uneven Distribution of the Effects of Specific Factors* (Southern California Education Monographs, No. 12; Los Angeles: Univ. of Southern California Press, 1941). George D. Spache, "Estimating Reading Capacity," in Helen M. Robinson (ed.), *Evaluation of Reading* (Chicago: Univ. of Chicago Press, 1958), pp. 15–200. Carol Winkley, "Building Staff Competence in Identifying Underachievers," in H. Alan Robinson (ed.), *The Underachiever in Reading* (Chicago: Univ. of Chicago Press, 1962), pp. 155–62.

6. Teacher observation of behavior in the class setting. Teacher evaluation is very important to the consultant and the remedial reading teacher. Classroom teachers, having seen students in a variety of situations, may have clear impressions and judgments that will contribute much to a diagnosis. A very basic principle underlying remediation is the need for close cooperation between the remedial program and the regular classroom program.

7. Interviews with the student or his parents for the specific purpose of discussing reading needs, interests, and attitudes.

8. Inventories aimed at the student's interests and attitudes toward reading.

After the analysis of the reading of a given student has been completed and all contributing factors carefully scrutinized, a meaningful synthesis must be made. The diagnostician conveys this information along with recommendations to the staff members working with the student.

Diagnosis is continuous. Students' needs change. Constant reevaluation must be made in order to discover the kinds of changes in the students' growth and the changes that will be necessary in the instructional procedures. The reading consultant should perform the job of coordinator to assure the continuity of the ongoing school program and to coordinate communication among classroom teachers, remedial reading teachers, and other staff members concerned.

Providing for Remedial Instruction

A great deal of care must be exercised in scheduling students for remedial work in order not to "step on toes" or inconvenience teachers. It is important, therefore, that the reading consultant and the remedial reading teachers become thoroughly acquainted with the daily program. Even then, there may be conflicts between remedial schedules and the schedules of homeroom or other classes. It is impossible to meet every situation ideally, and compromises will in many cases need to be worked out with the help of the administrators and teachers. It may also be helpful to discuss some of the problems with the students involved, in an effort to have them understand the total situation and take some initiative for their own programs.

Even though compromises are often necessary, it must be kept in mind that reading is fundamental to success in school. For a large number of students, remedial reading may play a vital role in their lives. The remedial reading class is not something to fit in when convenient. It should have a high priority. The reading consultant is largely responsible for promoting a desirable attitude on the part of the staff and students toward the remedial reading program. He must be able to convey the feeling that adjustments in scheduling can be made for the good of the student and the total program, but at the same time he must not permit the remedial reading program to be considered an extra frill.

Scheduling help for the retarded reader can be accomplished in many ways. It is important that scheduling be flexible to allow for the changing needs of students. The following are some of the most commonly used methods.

CORRECTIVE INSTRUCTION IN REGULAR CLASSROOMS. The regular classroom teacher can be expected to give corrective instruction to moderately disabled readers, or to those students who show good reading ability on standardized tests but who do not use their ability in daily reading, and to students whose general reading scores are satisfactory but who are deficient in certain skills. Although these students are a part of the regular developmental program, the teacher (with the help of the consultant) can adjust material to their levels and emphasize the needed skills.

SPECIAL REMEDIAL CLASSES. Special remedial classes may be conducted either by a regular teacher who has specialized training in the teaching of reading or by a remedial reading teacher. The consultant will coordinate this work by assisting with diagnoses, suggesting remedial procedures to be used with specific students, obtaining materials for instruction, and helping the teachers to evaluate student progress.

In addition, the reading consultant will be concerned with the scheduling of students for remedial instruction. The following are some useful ways of organizing for remedial instruction.

1. Groups of students can be dismissed at scheduled times for special reading instruction conducted by the remedial reading teacher.
2. Classes can be doubled up at different times to free a teacher for remedial reading instruction.
3. Students can be assigned to receive instruction during a regular study period.
4. Students can be taken from subject-matter classes where their reading weakness is a serious handicap.
5. Remedial instruction can be provided before school begins in the morning or after the regular dismissal time.
6. It can be provided during the regular homeroom period of the day or during the activity period.
7. Double English classes can be organized so that students needing help may receive remedial instruction while other students participate in enrichment activities or special individual projects.

8. Certain sections of English classes can be organized for retarded readers needing special help.

9. The remedial teacher can go into the classroom and provide remedial instruction while the majority of the class receives instruction with the regular classroom teacher.

TIPS

SCHEDULING REMEDIAL INSTRUCTION

1. The bases for selection and scheduling must be fully explained to all teachers.

2. Every effort should be made to screen and select students for remedial instruction during the spring so that no time is lost in the fall.

3. Spring or summer scheduling of remedial classes, especially at the secondary level, will permit grouping on the basis of need and assure a priority spot in the master schedule.

4. Groups will fluctuate in size, depending on need and physical facilities. There is no one best size. Some students will need individual tutoring for a time. Most remedial groups, however, should not contain more than seven students. Occasionally special instruction may be given for a limited time to students with a common reading deficiency, and the group may be of normal class size.

5. Instruction should last from thirty to forty-five minutes, depending on age, concentration ability, and reading weaknesses.

6. Instruction should take place daily when feasible. It should rarely be given less than three times a week. The scheduling of remedial cases once a week is difficult to justify.

READING CLINICS. Reading clinics may be found in many colleges and universities, but some are integral parts of school systems. If the school system has a reading clinic, the consultant may direct it or coordinate its activities with the rest of the program.

TEACHING BY THE CONSULTANT. Individual or group teaching may be done by the consultant. The consultant may work with a limited number of the most severely retarded readers. However, a word of caution is necessary: teaching students is not the *primary* function of a reading consultant.

SUMMER READING PROGRAMS. Summer school offers the retarded reader an additional opportunity to acquire help in reading. Summer reading programs may include remedial reading classes or may offer tutoring to individual students. The reading consultant should offer the same help to the teacher involved in the summer program as he does to the teacher of the regular school year. If the consultant is expected to help with both regular sessions and summer sessions, he should be compensated for this full-year program.

FOR FURTHER READING

BOND, GUY L., and TINKER, MILES A. *Reading Difficulties: Their Diagnosis and Correction*. New York: Appleton-Century-Crofts, 1957. Chaps. 7–16.

HARRIS, ALBERT J. *How to Increase Reading Ability*. 4th ed. New York: Longmans, Green, 1961. Chap. 11.

National Society for the Study of Education. *Development in and Through Reading*. (60th Yearbook, Part I.) Chicago: Univ. of Chicago Press, 1961. Chap. 20 (by HELEN M. ROBINSON).

ROBINSON, H. ALAN (ed.). *The Underachiever in Reading*. Chicago: Univ. of Chicago Press, 1962.

SCHUBERT, DELWYN A., and TORGERSON, THEODORE L. *Improving Reading in the Elementary School*. Dubuque, Iowa: Wm. C. Brown, 1963. Chaps. 1, 2.

CHAPTER 7

EVALUATION

Although partially treated in Chapters 3 and 4, evaluation is so important to the reading consultant and to the total reading program that this chapter focuses attention on several more facets of the problem. Evaluation of the reading program is the process of determining the extent to which objectives sought have been achieved. It is essential that the reading consultant, working with various school personnel, clearly formulate objectives of the reading program before choosing tools for evaluation purposes. The reading consultant and the school staff will formulate objectives concerned with both the overall reading program (for example, "a wholesome attitude toward reading resulting from a multitude of satisfying experiences with reading") and specific aspects of the program (for example, "the ability to grasp the literal meaning of a specific passage"). When objectives have been agreed upon, the reading consultant, with other members of the staff, will determine the specific needs and times for evaluation, as well as the particular tools to be used.

Purposes of Evaluation

There are two major purposes for evaluating. First, evaluation of the *total* reading program is essential in order to ensure that the adopted objectives of the program are being met. In this overall evaluation, consideration must be given to the teaching methods, the materials, the measuring instruments, and the students' ability to fulfill the objectives. What the consultant learns from such an evaluation could lead to changes in methods, materials, and measuring instruments and even in the adopted objectives.

A second purpose for evaluating is to ascertain the progress of students in reading. This may be accomplished through a school survey, the survey of an individual class, or the testing of an individual student. *The school survey is used—*

1. To determine the common strengths and weaknesses or the levels of reading achievement for the total student body.

2. To screen the students in order to identify those who need further diagnosis and possibly remedial help.

3. To provide data for important studies of the school.

4. To evaluate all students' abilities to use certain skills that have been emphasized in the reading program.

The *survey of individual classes* may be used—

To help teachers determine the reading achievement or overall strengths and weaknesses of individuals in a particular class.

To help teachers in grouping students for instructional purposes.

To assist teachers in the selection of appropriate instructional materials.

To screen students in order to locate those who may need further diagnosis and remedial treatment.

To determine mastery of specific skills taught in class.

The *testing of an individual student* may be conducted—

To determine his reading level or overall strengths and weaknesses upon entering the school system so that he may be placed with the proper instructional group.

To give the student a thorough diagnosis as a possible prelude to remedial work.

To test his mastery of a group of specific skills.

Evaluation is not a step that can be accomplished once at the beginning of a program and then again at the end of the school year or the start of the next year. Ruth Strang suggests that—

1. Evaluation should be continuous rather than periodic.
2. It should be a part of the instructional program, not apart from it.
3. It should obtain evidence on the extent to which the stated objectives have been achieved.
4. In obtaining this evidence, it should use both formal and informal methods.
5. The data collected should be used for the improvement of program and procedures.
6. Evaluation of a reading program should be carried on by a team that includes administrators, reading consultants, other specialists, teachers, students, and parents.
7. Increasing emphasis should be placed on self-appraisal as the student grows older.[12]

[12]Ruth Strang, "Evaluation of Development in and Through Reading," in *Development in and Through Reading* (60th Yearbook of the National Society for the Study of Education, Part I), pp. 381–82.

Tools of Evaluation

The reading consultant should know how to use a variety of evaluation tools, such as tests, check sheets, questionnaires, interviews, inventories, observations, and surveys. The procedures may be formal or informal, depending on needs and purposes. The area evaluated may be reading itself or one of the various factors related to reading, such as intelligence, vision, or general academic achievement.

STANDARDIZED READING TESTS. Three kinds of standardized reading test essentially make up the group of formal evaluation tools. *Survey tests* are used to assess the reading achievement of students in entire states, cities, school systems, individual schools, or individual classrooms, or even the reading achievement of individual students. Yielding only one or two scores, most often in vocabulary and paragraph comprehension, such tests may give rough indications of reading level but cannot be used for diagnostic purposes. The Metropolitan and Stanford tests and STEP (Sequential Tests of Educational Progress) are among the survey tests most frequently used.

Semidiagnostic tests are used for purposes similar to those of the survey tests, except that they usually yield three or more subscores. These subscores—though derived from test sections too brief to provide really reliable diagnostic data—do suggest possible strengths or deficiencies that may be further diagnosed. These tests often add a rate-of-reading section to sections on vocabulary and word recognition, and they may also attempt to measure a variety of other factors. Such tests include the California Reading Tests, the Cooperative English Tests, the Gates Reading Survey, and the Iowa Silent Reading Tests.

Diagnostic tests are used primarily for individuals having problems with reading, although some may be used with groups to better appraise class needs. These tests probe specific skill areas in some depth in order to determine needs and to aid in setting up a remedial program. The Van Wagenen Analytical Reading Scales, the Spache Diagnostic Reading Scales, and the McCullough Word Analysis Tests are representative of this group.

INTELLIGENCE TESTS. Since most of the available evidence suggests that reading is related to learning capacity—especially as the reader matures—the reading consultant needs to be concerned with intelligence tests. Although he may realize the weaknesses of such tests and know that capacity can be judged in many other ways, intelligence tests do give some indication of potential. Whenever possible—but certainly when severe reading problems are evident—a student should be given an individual intelligence test (preferably a Wechsler Intelligence Scale or the Revised Stanford-Binet, Form L-M); this test should be administered by a *trained* examiner.

When an individual test cannot be given, the reading consultant will need to be sure that the group intelligence test is carefully selected and carefully interpreted. For students with reading difficulties the group intelligence test may well be a test of reading ability rather than of intelligence. Group intelligence tests yielding *both* verbal and nonverbal scores are the most useful, for a nonverbal or performance score may be indicative of potential once the reading problems are overcome.

OTHER FORMAL TESTS. Numerous tests in areas other than reading or intelligence should be familiar to the reading consultant, for he will sometimes be called upon to administer them or interpret their results. *General achievement tests*—such as the SRA, California, Stanford, Iowa, and Metropolitan tests—may treat reading, spelling, language, social studies, science, mathematics, and study skills. They give rough indications of achievement in a number of these areas and add to information gathered about reading achievement and intelligence. *Readiness tests,* such as the Gates, Metropolitan, and Lee-Clark tests, are normally given in kindergarten or grade 1 to ascertain the degree of readiness for reading.

Vitally important to reading consultants are *vision and hearing tests;* every student should be given thorough visual and auditory screenings. However, some words of warning are appropriate here. First, visual examinations should be conducted by vision specialists or by reading specialists who understand school problems and the need for near-point efficiency. (Some recommended instruments for visual screening are the Keystone Visual Survey Test, the Bausch and Lomb Ortho-Rater, and the Massachusetts Vision Test. The Snellen test used so frequently in our schools is inadequate.) Second, auditory examinations should include a hearing acuity test with a pure tone audiometer. Third, both visual and auditory discrimination should be measured carefully, so that training may be related to specific needs.

Criteria for the Selection of Standardized Tests

The reading consultant should observe several criteria in selecting standardized tests. First, there is *validity,* which is the degree to which a particular standardized test measures what it purports to measure. The test should either obtain a sample of the kind of behavior stated in the objectives or be highly related to such expected behavior. If the test does not have high validity in the area it is supposed to measure, then it should be discarded as unsuitable. To judge the validity of a new test, the consultant should be familiar with the statements made in the manual and compare the test's results with those of a test known to be valid as well as with the norms of the test populations used. He may see how experts in the field have rated the test by consulting the evaluations appearing in *The Mental Measurements Yearbooks,* which indicate how much research was done on the validity of a given test and on what type of population the norms were standardized.

While validity refers to appropriateness, the second criterion, *reliability*, refers to consistency of accuracy. If a test is reliable, it should yield the same results with comparable forms of the same test and upon repeated administration of the test.

Objectivity, another criterion, refers to the degree to which a standardized test can be scored with a minimum of individual judgment as to the correctness or incorrectness of answers to the test questions. If questions can have more than one correct answer or if questions are subject to various interpretations, then the objectivity of the test is subject to criticism.

Usability, the final criterion, comprises a number of practical considerations that can distinguish highly usable tests from impractical ones. First, the *cost of the test* must obviously be within reason in terms of the utility of its results. The consultant should ask himself what benefits the administration will gain. Second, the test should be judged as to its *ease of administration and scoring*. Standardized tests must be accompanied by a manual of clear and precise directions that are easy to follow. If the test is timed, the exact amount of time should stand out clearly in the directions. Usually tests with few subscores can be administered and scored more easily than those with many subscores. The fact that some tests can be machine-scored while others are self-scoring is an important matter to consider when large numbers of tests must be quickly processed. Third, the *printing and format* of the test should be such that the student finds the test clearly outlined and readable. Finally, the consultant should determine the *adequacy of the stated norms*. It is important that the section on norms in the manual be read carefully to determine whether the samples on which the norms were established are representative. Ideally, the test should fit the character of the reading consultant's school system very closely; but if it does not, differences should be accounted for in comparing one's student body with the test population.

The reading consultant will find it desirable and helpful to become part of the test selection committee or, where such a committee does not exist, to organize one if test selection is his responsibility. Tests chosen in the light of the above criteria and considered in relation to the specific school objectives have more chance of contributing to evaluations of significance.

An Appraisal of Standardized Tests

MERITS OF STANDARDIZED TESTS. Like other tools of teaching, standardized tests can be appraised in terms of both their form and their results. In their form—that is, their structure and operation—these tests have very important advantages: (1) their content is usually determined by careful design; (2) there are often parallel forms for comparison; (3) they permit many children to be tested simultaneously; and (4) they are objective in administering and scoring. In many schools, standardized tests are the first step in identifying those students who are below grade level and who are in need of further diagnosis.

Standardized tests are particularly useful in measuring the wide range of reading levels in a class, school, or school system. They also provide standards for comparing students on a nationwide basis. Standardized tests make a valuable contribution to modern education by demonstrating rather clearly that children differ. They provide standards for making improvements in school programs in the areas of curriculum, school and classroom organization, and methods and materials of instruction.

LIMITATIONS OF STANDARDIZED TESTS. Although they can be extremely valuable to reading consultants, standardized tests do have several limitations. In addition to sometimes not measuring what they purport to measure, such tests are simply unsatisfactory for measuring certain things. They are unable to measure well such intangible aspects of learning as interest, attitude, appreciation, determination, and purpose. They often fail to diagnose the specific needs of children who, though adept at dealing with formal tests, are unable to apply the same skill in their daily work; the obvious inference is that ability to answer questions on a test does not ensure successful application in class. Moreover, the various tests differ greatly in content, and standardized norms of all tests are not suited to all groups of children.

Whatever the intrinsic merits or defects of standardized tests, there is the danger that they may be misused or misapplied: (1) they may, inappropriately, be used to compare the standards of different class groups, schools, or systems; (2) they may be used not to appraise student performance but to rate the effectiveness of teachers; (3) there may be a tendency to rely too heavily on one test result rather than on a series of scores obtained over the years; (4) the results of one test may be used to decide the fate of an individual without proper consideration of other important data; (5) scores on tests may be indiscriminately used as if they were—when, in fact, they are not—absolutely valid indications of an individual's reading level; (6) tests may be selected without due concern for the purposes to be served in administering the tests.

FACTORS TO CONSIDER IN ADMINISTERING AND SCORING TESTS. Several environmental and procedural conditions, both in administering and scoring standardized tests, influence the outcome of test scores. Factors with which teachers and consultants should be particularly concerned are the following:

1. *Physical surroundings.* The class atmosphere should be conducive to testing. The test administrator should ask himself such questions as "Has the classroom been free of interruptions or unusual noises during the testing?"

or "Has the room temperature been satisfactory?"

2. *Mental and physical condition of the individual.* Many students "freeze" in the testing situation; some may even be physically ill at the time of testing. Thus the administrator should guard against treating testing as if it were an all-important means of evaluation or a life-or-death matter in the school.

3. *Test format.* The general appearance of a test may be so formidable as to discourage the slow or retarded reader. The organization of terms and typography can influence a pupil's attitude toward a test.

4. *Time limits.* Too frequently, rate tests of one to three minutes duration tend to test speed of reaction rather than speed of reading comprehension.

5. *Pupils' experience with one type of test.* Pupils may acquire a certain amount of test-taking sophistication and experience that will enhance their test scores.

6. *Teacher preparation.* Unfortunately, not all teachers who administer tests read the manual. Some of the variations from standard procedures seriously affect the use of the norms supplied. It is the responsibility of the reading consultant to see that teachers are ready before a test is administered.

7. *Following directions.* Both teachers and students can make errors in following directions. Some teachers will ignore time limits, while some students will fail to turn to the correct page or begin with the proper item. The complexity or ambiguity of directions may present more of a problem than the actual test selections.

8. *Scoring by teachers.* Apart from simple arithmetical errors, some teachers may ignore or forget the special scoring instructions. The reading consultant who "knows the test" will want to emphasize scoring instructions.

9. *Guessing.* Reading consultants have still to learn how to distinguish the intelligent guesses of students from their wild guesses. However, it is profitable for the scorer to think the matter through and attempt to determine how the correct answer was chosen.

Rather than attempt to supply a list of standardized tests and to evaluate them for our readers, we recommend that the reading consultant become familiar with the following reference works.

BUROS, OSCAR KRISEN (ed.). *The Fourth Mental Measurements Yearbook.* Highland Park, N.J.: Gryphon Press, 1953.

————. *The Fifth Mental Measurements Yearbook.* Highland Park, N. J.: Gryphon Press, 1959. These *Mental Measurements Yearbooks* are the primary references for evaluating standardized tests. Before any recommendations for test use are made, these volumes should be consulted.

———. *Tests in Print.* Highland Park, N.J.: Gryphon Press, 1961.

GARRETT, HENRY E. *Testing for Teachers.* New York: American Book, 1959. This volume contains simple, clear explanations and illustrations of the terms commonly used in testing and evaluation.

HARRIS, ALBERT J. *How to Increase Reading Ability.* 4th ed. New York: McKay, 1961. See Appendix A for "An Alphabetical List of Tests," which includes brief descriptions of subtests, working times, and prices.

THORNDIKE, ROBERT L., and HAGEN, ELIZABETH. *Measurement and Evaluation in Psychology and Education.* 2d ed. New York: Wiley, 1961. See Appendix iii (pp. 571–91) for a description and evaluation of general intelligence tests, aptitude tests, reading tests, elementary and high school achievement batteries, and interest inventories.

Informal Measures

Informal measures may be used (1) to diagnose aspects of reading achievement *not* measured by standardized tests, such as the ability to organize and retain ideas after reading an extended passage; (2) to learn about aspects of reading ability *inadequately* measured by standardized tests, such as the ability to draw conclusions or the ability to react to what is read; (3) to serve as a check on the results of a standardized test given to a particular individual; or (4) to measure the less tangible aspects of reading, such as the approach to a textbook assignment, the techniques of notetaking, or interests and attitudes.

The important informal measures include inventories, special skill tests, questionnaires, checklists, interviews, observations through teaching, analyses of work samples, and self-appraisal techniques. Most of these measures are thoroughly discussed in a number of professional books; see particularly Ruth Strang, *Diagnostic Teaching of Reading* (New York: McGraw-Hill, 1964), and Mary C. Austin, Clifford L. Bush, and Mildred H. Huebner, *Reading Evaluation* (New York: Ronald Press, 1961).

THE INFORMAL READING INVENTORY. The informal measure that is used most widely and that is probably of greatest service in testing the functional reading levels of students is the informal reading inventory (IRI). There are different versions of such an inventory—see, for example, Nila Banton Smith's two volumes of *Graded Selections for Informal Reading Diagnosis* (New York: New York Univ. Press, 1963); Chapter 21 of Emmett A. Bett's *Foundations of Reading Instruction* (New York: American Book, 1957); and the *Diagnostic Reading Scales* (Monterey, Calif.: California Test Bureau, 1961)—but essentially IRI is an informal diagnostic tool usually based on selections from a series of graded books and used to determine levels of reading ability for individual students.

An IRI is best prepared by a committee of teachers representing different grade levels. It may be developed from a set of graded readers or from a set of graded content-area textbooks. Two selections may be taken from each level, one to be read orally by the student and the other silently; but they should be representative of the general difficulty of the book from which they are excerpted. The selections then may be printed or duplicated along with prepared questions that check vocabulary knowledge and such comprehension skills as recognizing main ideas and supporting details, organization, and inferences and conclusions to be gained from the reading.

The IRI is administered individually to each student. The student is asked to begin reading at a level where he will experience little or no difficulty. The highest level at which he can read with ease is his *independent level*. He continues then to the level where the material is somewhat difficult but challenging (*instructional level*) and then to those materials obviously too difficult for him (*frustration level*). The student reads directly from the book, while the examiner notes errors on a mimeographed copy. A stopwatch may be used to check both oral and silent reading rates. Details such as finger pointing, vocalizations, mispronunciations, substitutions, omissions, repetitions, and insertions are recorded.

Since the purpose of the IRI is to test specific strengths and weaknesses of the individual's reading at many levels, the teacher should derive concrete information about the student's word analysis and comprehension skills at progressive levels of difficulty. However, it must be emphasized that the IRI is as good as the teachers who prepare it and as accurate as the teachers who administer it. Whenever possible, the teacher should supplement his judgment with the results of standardized tests.

In general, standardized silent-reading tests will give scores higher than the instructional levels obtained on an IRI. When there is a discrepancy of more than a year between the results of a standardized test and the results of an IRI, the IRI should be given preference (assuming, of course, that it has been carefully constructed and intelligently administered).

The percentages given in the criteria below may be used as guides to determine levels of reading. It must be remembered, however, that the *teacher's judgment* of the type and frequency of error is more important than the routine computation of a percentage.

CRITERIA FOR INDEPENDENT LEVEL   *-90% overall*

    A. 90–100 percent comprehension

    B. 98–100 percent accuracy in word attack

    C. Fluent oral reading

    D. Relative freedom from head movements, finger pointing, excessive vocalization, and tenseness

    E. General feeling that this is the level where the student can read on his own with enjoyment and without difficulty

CRITERIA FOR INSTRUCTIONAL LEVEL

A. 70–85 percent comprehension

B. 95–97 percent accuracy in word attack

C. Relatively fluent oral reading

D. Relative freedom from head movements, finger pointing, excessive vocalization, and tenseness

E. General feeling that this is the level where the student needs some help but where he is not frustrated

CRITERIA FOR FRUSTRATION LEVEL

A. 65 percent or below in comprehension

B. 94 percent or below in word attack

C. Slow, hesitant, word-by-word oral reading

D. Excessive head movements, finger pointing, vocalization, or tenseness

E. General feeling that the reading is too difficult and that the student should not attempt to read or learn at this frustrating level

CRITERIA FOR INTERPRETATION OF ORAL READING[13]

Counting of errors:

Minus 1 point for each error

A. Major substitutions

    1. Configurational errors

    2. Contextual errors

B. Mispronunciations

C. Words unknown

D. Omission of key words (any word whose omission would alter meaning)

Minus ½ point for each error

A. Addition or omission of inflectional endings

B. Repetitions

C. Addition or omission of articles, prepositions, conjunctions, or personal pronouns (relatively unimportant words)

D. Other mistaken insertions

---

[13]The "Criteria for Interpretation of Oral Reading" were developed at the Hofstra University Reading Clinic.

NOTE: (1) Spontaneous corrections are not to be counted as errors. (2) No words should be pronounced by the examiner; otherwise comprehension will be affected. If the student balks at a word and refuses to go on, then it is permissible for the examiner to pronounce the word. However, if the pronunciation of the word affects comprehension, the student should not be given credit for a correct answer.

TEACHER-MADE TESTS. Teachers, of course, may employ numerous kinds of informal tests other than the IRI—for example, selections from books, workbook pages, or mimeographed sheets to test specific skills. For an example of a reading skills test in a content area, see Ruth Strang and Dorothy K. Bracken, *Making Better Readers* (Boston: Heath, 1957), pp. 222–33. Some of the advantages of teacher-made tests are that (1) they test the student's progress in skills stressed by the teacher but omitted in standardized tests; (2) they assist in appraising reading growth in line with specific reading objectives; (3) they help determine growth over a short period of time; (4) they point out areas of general class weakness; (5) they compare one student with the others in his class rather than with the general population; (6) they serve as teaching or review exercises and allow students to observe and study their errors after marking; (7) they provide students with frequent and helpful experience in following directions; and (8) they provide the teacher with a quick method of evaluating the effectiveness of his teaching methods.

OTHER INFORMAL MEASURES. One excellent example of an informal measure is the file folder record of student achievement. Although this folder—which is prepared for a clinical situation—may be too detailed for class use, it considers important aspects of reading not measured by formal or informal tests and could be adapted for the classroom. See pp. 29–32.

Some informal measure that offers a *diagnosis of study skills* is also important; indeed, a teacher's primary concern is the study skills of his students. Many students who in a standardized reading test can answer questions about a short paragraph cannot attack a longer selection successfully. They are unable to organize as they read, and they fail to relate significant details to the main ideas. Many of them do not know how to skim or how to look for signal or cue words. They fail to adjust their rate to their purpose and to the difficulty of the reading selection.

To diagnose these study skills, a teacher may administer the following informal test during the regular class period at the beginning of the school term: the entire class is given twenty to thirty minutes to read a chapter (or portions of a chapter) from a social science text in preparation for a test. Paper is supplied for notetaking, and the students may use their notes in answering the subsequent questions, but the students may not refer to the chapter itself once the reading time is up. The teacher may observe carefully the various approaches to this type of assignment and make comments later on. These are some of the skills checked by this kind of informal test: (1) use of survey techniques, (2) notetaking, (3) outlining, (4) use of signal words, (5) summarizing, and (6) making inferences. A review of the results of this kind of test might well serve as a starting point for a series of lessons on study skills.

FOR FURTHER READING

BOND, GUY L., and TINKER, MILES A. *Reading Difficulties: Their Diagnosis and Correction.* New York: Appleton-Century-Crofts, 1957.

CRONBACH, LEE J. *Essentials of Psychological Testing.* 2d ed. New York: Harper, 1960.

GARRETT, HENRY E. *Testing for Teachers.* New York: American Book, 1959.

Testing Guide for Teachers. New York: Educational Records Bureau, 1961.

THORNDIKE, ROBERT L., and HAGEN, ELIZABETH. *Measurement and Evaluation in Psychology and Education.* New York: John Wiley, 1961.

GUIDELINES FOR A GOOD READING PROGRAM

Criteria for a Sound Reading Program in the Elementary School[14]

1. A good reading program in an elementary school is consciously directed toward specific valid ends which have been agreed upon by the entire school staff. Widely accepted ends are: rich and varied experiences through reading; broadening interests and improved tastes in reading; enjoyment through reading; increased personal and social adjustment; curiosity concerning the ideas given in the reading material; resourcefulness in using reading to satisfy one's purposes; and growth in the fundamental reading abilities, such as ability to recognize the words, to understand the meanings of words, to comprehend and interpret what is read, to locate references bearing on a problem, and to organize ideas gathered from different sources.

2. A good reading program coordinates reading activities with other aids to child development.

3. It recognizes that the child's development in reading is closely associated with his development in other language arts.

4. At any given level the program is part of a well-worked-out, larger reading program extending through all the elementary and secondary school grades.

5. It provides varied instruction and flexible requirements as a means of making adequate adjustments to the widely different reading needs of the pupils.

6. It affords, at each level of advancement, adequate guidance of reading in all the various aspects of a broad program of instruction—basic instruction in reading, reading in the content fields, literature, and recreational or free reading.

7. It makes special provisions for supplying the reading needs of pupils with extreme reading disability—in other words, the small proportion of pupils whose needs cannot be satisfied through a strong developmental program.

8. It provides for frequent evaluation of the outcomes of the program and for such revisions as will strengthen the weaknesses discovered.

[14]Formulated by Gertrude Whipple in "Characteristics of a Sound Reading Program," *Reading in the Elementary School* (National Society for the Study of Education, 48th Yearbook, Part 2, 1949). For a detailed description of each criterion, turn to pages 34–38 of the Yearbook.

Criteria for a Sound Reading Program in High School and College[15]

1. A sound reading program is planned cooperatively by the total staff or by an adequate representation of the staff.

2. It is directed toward specific goals leading to independence in reading.

3. It is balanced and is therefore concerned with all aspects of reading.

4. It provides for basic skill instruction with directed application to a variety of reading situations.

5. It provides for the individual reading needs of all students, on a basis of adequate diagnosis.

6. It adjusts instruction and materials to those individual needs.

7. It makes special provision for relieving the reading needs of the severely retarded reader who cannot obtain all the help he needs through normal classroom instruction.

8. It endeavors to make students cognizant of their strengths, weaknesses, and goals through a continuous evaluation program.

9. It allows subject-matter teachers to teach the reading skills pertinent to their own subjects.

10. It makes in-service training a continuing factor in the reading program.

11. It is understood by students, school personnel, parents, and the community at large.

12. It is continuously evaluated in terms of specific goals.

Reading Skills Checklist

Reading skills must be taught. It is not enough to say to the average elementary or secondary student, "Here is an interesting book. Read it." Even though there is no one best program for the systematic development of skills, there is a need for *carefully planned, definite instruction.*

The most successful teaching of skills occurs when boys and girls are aware of a need for a certain skill, such as the techniques of skimming in the preparation for an exam, or the use of footnotes and bibliographies in the preparation of a term report. However, many needed skills may not be directly related to the immediate classroom activity or unit. The teacher must recognize that certain skill needs will eventually arise and that it may be more economical of time and effort to teach a skill without insisting that the specific need be present.

The outline that follows is designed to give the teacher a quick general picture of the entire scope of the skills. The grade placement of these skills depends upon the maturity of the students and on their previous learnings.

[15] Suggested by Virginia Anderson, Margarethe Livesay, and H. Alan Robinson.

Skills of word attack
1. Visual clues (use of pictures, charts, diagrams, etc., for meaning)
2. Context (or meaning in the sentence)
3. Configuration (the general appearance of the word as an aid to quick recognition and identification of the word)
4. Structural analysis (knowledge of root words, prefixes, suffixes, inflectional endings, syllabication)
5. Phonetic analysis (process of associating appropriate sounds with the printed letter forms—*i.e.,* recognizing consonants, consonant blends, vowels, and vowel combinations)
6. The dictionary (for meaning, pronunciation, finding a better word, spelling, and sometimes word derivations)

Comprehension skills
1. Reading to get general significance (main idea or ideas)
2. Noting details
3. Making judgments (reading critically)
4. Comparing and contrasting
5. Making inferences and drawing conclusions
6. Evaluating (fact-fiction; fact-propaganda)

NOTE: The following skills all involve comprehension but are placed in separate categories.

Study skills
1. Adapting skills to materials
2. Following directions
3. Notemaking and outlining
4. Summarizing
5. Skimming
6. Reading to remember

Locational skills
1. Using dictionary, reference books, etc.
2. Using table of contents, indexes, glossary
3. Using locational skills in specific volumes (*Readers' Guide, Who's Who, World Almanac,* etc.)
4. Using maps, atlas, charts, graphs
5. Using illustrations, symbols, abbreviations
6. Using footnotes, bibliographies
7. Appraising subject; estimating sources

Appreciation skills
1. Visualizing enriching imagery
2. Recognizing the author's intent and mood
3. Appreciating literary style, figures of speech

4. Understanding semantics (science of word meanings)
5. Understanding approaches to poetry, drama, the novel, the essay, and other literary forms

NOTE: There is nothing definitive about these classifications. More than one hundred skills have been listed in various textbooks on reading. These skills have here been condensed to thirty. However, they may well provide a frame of reference for clearer understanding of the skills. A teacher who recognizes the individual problems and general maturity of students must decide for himself the grade placement of each skill and the emphasis to be placed on it.

Criteria for Selecting and Evaluating Reading Materials

1. Materials should be selected and evaluated for suitability in achieving the objectives of a reading program.

2. Materials should be selected and evaluated in relation to a plan for continuous development. Materials directed toward reading instruction should provide for development of a systematic sequence of skills.

3. Materials used for skill development in supplementing a basic program must be specifically related to the particular skill in which a given student or group of students is deficient.

4. Materials should be at the appropriate level of difficulty (in terms of both skill and personal maturity) for the students concerned.

5. Although all materials will not be of equal interest to all students, materials should be chosen and evaluated in accordance with realistic needs and interests of the student or group of students concerned.

6. Materials should be selected and evaluated in relation to broadening the students' intellectual and emotional experiences.

7. Practice materials should be appropriate to the purpose for which they are used and should maintain a balance between success and challenge.

8. Materials should be varied enough in content, type, length, interest, and point of view so that students may have many different kinds of reading experiences, including abundant opportunities for voluntary reading.

9. The authors of materials for both instructional and recreational uses should be experts in their field; authors of instructional materials, in particular, should also be aware of the developmental needs and interests of students.

10. Students should have the opportunity to select and evaluate materials. These judgments by students are of value to the teacher in his own selection and evaluation of reading materials.

Reading: How the Parent Can Help[16]

NOTE: The New York City schools have prepared a list of suggestions for parents that seems particularly useful. It is reproduced here to serve as a guide to the reading consultant.

Teaching reading is an important and difficult job in which both the school and the parent can cooperate.

Here are many ways in which you as a parent can help your child:

1. *Talk* to your child. Almost from the day he is born, a child is ready to express himself. At first, he will respond by cooing and gurgling. Later he will pick up a few words and sense the rhythm of language. Help him to add words to his speaking vocabulary. The more words he uses naturally in his ordinary conversation, the more words will have meaning for him when he sees them on the printed page.

2. *Listen* to your child. Children must have many opportunities to express themselves. Encourage your child to talk about things he has seen or done. The more the child talks, the better he is likely to read. Do pay attention when he is talking with you. Listen to your child read. Suggest that before he reads aloud to you, he should read the story to himself to be sure that he knows all the words. This makes listening to him read much more interesting to you.

3. *Read* to your child. Every time you read to him you are building an appreciation of books and reading. A child who has been read to is usually more anxious to read to himself. Reading becomes more important. Remember, his listening and interest levels are above his reading level.

4. *Help* him with his reading. Tell him the words if he's in the beginning stages of reading. Help him to work out the word if he's in a later stage by looking at the picture, skipping over the unknown word and reading the rest of the sentence to see whether this suggests a new word, and checking to see whether the word makes "sense" in the sentence. ("I was a pig" or "I saw a pig.")

5. *Teach* your child how to take care of books. He will then learn to regard books as friends.

6. *Take* him on trips. Even a short trip on the bus or subway will excite his curiosity and interest in the world around him. Point out interesting things and give him new words and meanings for words. The following places might be visited: Brooklyn Museum; Children's Museum; Metropolitan Museum of Art; Museum of Natural History; Prospect Park; Brooklyn Botanic Garden; Boat Trip around Manhattan Island; Boat Trip up the Hudson River; Hayden Planetarium; Brooklyn Public Library; Coney Island Animal Farm; Coney Island

[16]Prepared by the Division of Elementary Education, Board of Education of New York City.

Aquarium; Guided Bus Trip around Manhattan; Statue of Liberty; U.S. buildings; LaGuardia and Kennedy airports.

7. *Build up* a reading atmosphere at home. Have books, magazines, newspapers, etc. around the house. Let your child see you reading frequently. Tune in to thoughtful programs on the radio and television. Your child will tend to imitate his parents.

8. *Encourage* him to join the public library. Take him to the library at first. Don't tell him what books to select. If he is a poor reader, he may at first choose easy books. As he gains confidence, satisfaction, and improves in reading, he will choose more difficult books.

9. *Buy* games and puzzles for your child. These help your child learn shape and form and help him relate words to things. Anagrams, letter games, Scrabble, and lotto will help him with his spelling and reading. Jigsaw puzzles help a child recognize shape, because the puzzle piece must be matched to fit a space.

10. *Make games.* You can make simple word games by cutting words from a magazine and asking your child to match these words to a picture. Make word cards for troublesome words (*was, there, what, went,* etc.) and play a game with your child. How quickly can he learn the word and how many word cards can be removed from the pack because he really has learned them? What words should be added?

11. *Buy* books for your child. For birthdays and holidays, buy books when you can afford them. A child who owns a few good books is usually interested in reading. Try to get books at his reading grade level so he can read these books with fun and pleasure. Buy children's magazines too: *Children's Digest, Humpty Dumpty, Calling All Girls, Boys' Life,* etc.

12. *Praise* your child. Remember, reading is a difficult task. Don't forget to praise him when he succeeds. Don't expect him to know the word when you tell it once or twice or even ten or twenty times. Some normal children need to see a word many more times than this.

13. *Keep* your child well and rested. A child who has stayed up late to watch television shows the effect next day in his schoolwork. Cooperate with the school nurse and doctor in correcting his vision or hearing or nutritional defects.

14. *Give* your child responsibilities which he is capable of taking. This allows him to earn recognition and to get real satisfaction from accomplishments.

15. *See* that your child has good habits of attendance. When he is absent from school, he misses his work and may not be able to keep up with the class.

16. *Check* your child's report card. If he is having trouble with reading or any subject, consult his teacher to find out why and how you can help.

17. *Set aside* a regular time for homework. Give your child a definite place in which to work. Help him develop the habit of daily attention to homework routines.

18. *Guide* your child to better movie-going. Select radio and TV programs which will give him worthwhile information as well as entertainment. Check the newspaper listings for these programs.

19. *Accept* your child as he is. Don't compare him with his sister, brother, or friend. Encourage him to improve as much as he can.

20. *Show* a real interest in school. The parents' attitude is usually the child's. You and the teacher are partners in the important job of teaching your child to read. An *interested, relaxed, helpful* parent is a most valuable co-worker and *you* are the partners *we need*.

Remember: Children learn to read by reading. The more they read, the better readers they become!

INDEPENDENT ACTIVITIES FOR INDIVIDUALS OR SMALL GROUPS

General Concepts

INTRODUCTION

In large measure a teacher's success in his period of reading instruction hinges on his success in organizing the classroom so that those students not working at a given moment under his direct supervision are provided with independent activities. These activities should be carefully selected; they must be interesting and meaningful; they must lie within the student's range of performance; and they must be susceptible of evaluation by both teacher and student.

Two major considerations guide the organizing of independent activities: (1) the class should be organized so that the members know the rules and can move from one activity to another with a minimum of assistance and disturbance, and (2) the teacher should provide a varied range of activities. A bibliography of works dealing specifically with suggested activities is given at the end of this section. A beginning teacher will find that buying several of the books may be one of the wisest investments he ever makes.

ORGANIZATION

Many methods can be used in organizing the classroom. Following are a few examples.

An Agenda. On the chalkboard or other spot clearly visible to the entire class, the teacher each morning can post an agenda or list of activities for the morning or the full day. To provide for varying working rates, the teacher should list not only a minimum number of activities but also a supplementary number to challenge the bright, fast child. Minimum activities can be written with white chalk, and supplementary ones in colored chalk to signify this difference. Items should not be too specific but should allow for variability within the agenda. For example:

1. Copy the poem on writing paper [a poem previously placed on the board].
2. Work pages 10–11 in the number book [the concepts involved having been taught the preceding day].
3. Do the worksheet. [Separate worksheets for different groups or individuals can be placed in piles of boxes.]
4. Draw eight pictures of things that fly. [Show a sample of folded paper.]
5. Read a library book at your seat.

Interest Centers. Various areas in the room can be devoted to temporary or ongoing projects that students may work on after completion of their minimum tasks or in connection with them. These are examples of interest centers:

Science Corner
Library Corner
Programed Learning Materials
Art Corner or Painting Corner (clay, finger paints, papier-mâché)
Game Corner (puzzles, educational games)
Current Projects (class scrapbook, notebook, wall map)
Creative Writing (paper, pencils, ink, pictures, TV)
Cataloged Worksheets (Children should be made constantly aware of the
    kinds of activities on which they need practice in order to remove
    deficiencies.)
Arithmetic Corner (quiz or puzzle books, abacus, math games)
Listening Corner (outfitted with a record player or a tape recorder with ear-
    phones, if available)
Handicrafts Corner (scrap box, beads, shells, looms, pipe cleaners)
Dramatic Corner (puppet theater, cardboard "TV")

Treasure Box or Help-Yourself Box. A receptacle such as an accordion file, a cardboard box, a fishbowl, or a recipe box can contain sheets of paper or cards on which are given problems, situations, or directions for various activities. The child chooses one problem and accepts responsibility for carrying it out; the teacher checks only on the student's final accomplishment. The child can mark his own record on the index card, or the teacher can record achievements on a general chart in the room. To keep the help-yourself activities going, the teacher should maintain a continuous supply of new cards with new ideas.

The alert teacher should not only combine these various kinds of organized activities from time to time but also originate others. Variety is essential; no one method of organization used over and over again will ensure that students will continue to be motivated and eager. A few notes of caution might be helpful here: (1) Ground rules must be established early and enforced (for example, no more than three children should be allowed in the library corner at any one time). (2) Neophyte teachers should be warned that it is best to have only one "messy" activity going on at one time; that is, he should avoid combining work in papier-mâché, finger painting, and easel painting on the same day or the same week. (3) The teacher should arrange to have students turn in their work upon completion in order to facilitate checking; one or more "in" boxes serve this purpose nicely.

First Grade

In attempting to provide truly independent activities, the first-grade teacher is faced with special problems not faced by teachers of more mature students; thus, in the listing of suggested activities, grade 1 is here treated separately from grades 2 through 10. This list, like the one that follows for the later grades, is merely suggestive, not prescriptive; nor is it exhaustive of all possibilities. It is hoped that it will stimulate the teacher to improve and add to his own ideas.

1. On full sheets of manila paper or newsprint (or even on smaller sections after the students have learned to fold paper in halves, quarters, and eighths) the children can be asked to draw the following items in crayon (picture dictionaries might be used as aids).

Pictures of things that fly
Pictures of things with wheels
Pictures of things we eat
Pictures of things we wear
Pictures of things we do in summer
Pictures of things you do to help Mother
Pictures of things that rhyme with *can*
Pictures of happy words
Pictures of words that start like *Tom*
Pictures of things that go fast
Pictures of what you want to be when you grow up
Pictures of the story you liked best in our reading book
Pictures of Sally's friends
Pictures of the nursery rhyme you like best

2. On 9x12 piece of manila paper or newsprint, the child can be asked to print descriptive sentences (one to a sheet or section) taken from a story that has been read. The child chooses one sentence from a list and illustrates it ("Jim ran to meet Father at the train").

3. The child can be directed to poems on the chalkboard or in a poetry book and asked to choose one, copying it on writing paper, pasting the paper to a large sheet of drawing paper, and then drawing a picture of what is happening in the poem.

4. After listing words with only the beginning and ending letters given, the teacher can ask the child to write a real word by filling in the missing letters. This can also be done on drawing paper with a picture illustrating the written word.

5. On the chalkboard or on ditto sheets, a story can be printed with a number of words underlined. The child can then copy the story and put in a small drawing (rebus) to take the place of each underlined word.

6. On paper marked in half-inch or one-inch squares, the child can be directed to do the following.

Write the alphabet using large or small letters.
Color in the squares. (In the early fall, when the first-grader is still awkward
         at manipulating writing instruments, coloring work aids in the develop-
         ment of his muscle coordination.)
Write the numbers one through ten.
Write to fifty by twos.

7. On a chalkboard or ditto sheet, a pictorial item can be drawn with a part missing. The child can then be asked to copy and fill in the missing part (an animal with ear or tail missing, a house with no windows).

8. To help a child learn visually how to distinguish between various geometric designs, the teacher can cut colored pieces of paper into the shape of circles, triangles, squares, and rectangles. These geometric pieces can then be matched by the child to identical shapes outlined on a ditto sheet—the pieces of paper to be pasted in the appropriate outlines scattered on the paper. (The child can even be asked to do the original cutting of shaped pieces from colored paper previously printed with outlines of the geometric figures.)

9. On a ditto sheet, the teacher can print even rows of small geometric figures—a circle followed by a square, followed by a triangle, followed by a rectangle, followed by another circle, ad infinitum, the figures to be printed in no consistent order. With the sheet before him, the child then proceeds from the beginning of each row and with an identifying mark notes each recurrence of a specified figure—placing, for instance, a dot in each circle he comes across. The directions to the child, of course, can be varied: *O*'s can be written in squares, crosses in rectangles, and so on.

10. Using catalogs and old magazines, the teacher can instruct the child to find and cut out a picture of a small specified item—for example, something whose name begins with the letter *B*. Each picture can then be pasted on chart paper.

11. The child can be given a sheet of paper printed with rows of broken lines somewhat in the form of a labyrinth and be told to trace with a crayon the path that the "mouse" took to get to the "cheese." The path can be drawn with lines, dots, or circles.

12. After teaching a poem such as "The Toyman's Shop," the teacher can ask each child to draw a picture of one toy either named or alluded to in the poem and to print the name of the toy under his picture. The children might also draw a picture of the outside of the toy store, and the collection of the two pictures and the printed poem might be stapled into booklets.

13. Working with a list of words printed on a chalkboard or ditto sheet, the children might determine the category of things to which each word belongs (animal, plant, grownup, etc.) by writing the numeral 1, 2, or 3 beside it. *Classification*

14. On a chalkboard or ditto paper, the teacher can write several sentences taken from a story recently read or another story from a suitable book. The children may then be asked to find each sentence in the story and to write its page number in the blank preceding the sentence.

15. On the chalkboard, several sentences can be written with their word or-

der scrambled ("lost her children Mother Duck"). The child can then be asked to write the sentences in correct word order. *Comprehension*
Fargo - North Decoder

16. On the chalkboard can be written a series of questions or statements calling for comprehension ("Draw a picture of your pet"; "What can you buy at the grocery store?"). The child can then either draw a picture of the answer or write a word answer.

17. On the chalkboard can be written a series of sentences each of which contains a word or phrase making the sentence sound foolish ("Mary ate a wagon for breakfast"). The child should circle the nonsense words or phrases.

18. On a ditto sheet can be printed a series of sentences or very short stories, some sad and some funny. The child can be directed to distinguish the funny from the sad by drawing smiling and crying faces in the margin.

19. The teacher can select three or four sentences that one by one advance a familiar "story" or set of events from a beginning to a conclusion. The teacher lists these sentences out of their logical or chronological order, and the child is to determine their proper order, perhaps by numbering them. For example:

[3] Mary put the flowers in a vase.
[1] Mary went for a walk.
[2] Mary saw some pretty flowers.

20. Guided by a series of directions, the child can draw a picture on the chalkboard or on ditto paper. For example:

Draw a kitten.
Make a ball for the kitten.
Put a red collar on the kitten.
Put a blue dish near it for milk.

21. The teacher can draw a picture on the board (see illustration) and then ask each child to copy the picture on paper and label each object with the letter of the alphabet that represents the initial sound of the object's name. The child should be encouraged also to add objects of his own and to label them. The same activity can be designed to concentrate on a single letter sound rather than on many.

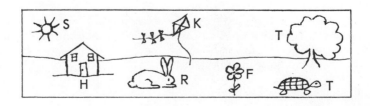

22. On the chalkboard, the teacher can draw pictures of a few objects—each object having a name containing a different vowel sound (a picture of a boat for the long *o;* a picture of a tree for the long *e*). Under these pictures can be written several words that contain vowel sounds identical with those in the names of the pictured items (*bone* and *home* for the vowel in *boat; feet* and *meat* for the vowel in *tree*). The students are asked to match the words with the pictures according to similar vowel sounds. (See illustration.)

23. The teacher can write a simple riddle on the board. The students copy the riddle, guess the subject of the riddle, write its name in the blank provided, and then draw its picture. For example:

I live in a pool.
I like to swim.
Cats like to eat me.
I am a [fish].

24. The students can be asked to draw a picture of an object whose name *rhymes* with the name of another pictured object or with a word given them.

25. On the chalkboard, the teacher can write a series of questions that can be answered on paper with a simple yes or no ("Can a boat eat?" "Can a rock talk?" "Can a tree swim?").

26. From the comic section of the newspaper, the teacher can select a strip of three or four frames to be clipped for class use. The frames are separated in order to give the students the problem of arranging the frames in their proper sequence.

Grades 2 through 10

In choosing an independent activity from a list of activities for several grade levels—like the list here of grades 2 through 10—any teacher must obviously adjust the activity to the maturity of his students. The difficulty of the concepts and the quantity of details involved would naturally increase in the higher grades.

As in the separate list for the first grade, the list here for grades 2 through 10 merely suggests the wide variety of possible activities and falls far short of exhausting the possibilities. Studying this list, however, the teacher may well be inspired to go on and invent other activities, both interesting and instructional.

1. From a supply of pictures from magazines (or pictures from the skillfully illustrated readiness books for the primary child), the teacher can choose one picture and ask the students to write a story about what is being depicted. They can be asked to tell who the characters are in the picture, what they are doing, and where they are going, and to determine the time of year, the setting, and the mood of the characters.

2. For reading research, the teacher can set forth a problematical situation such as the following: "Imagine that you are going to [a specified city, state, or nation] for a visit during the month of December. Tell what cities and countries you might pass through; what clothes you would need to take along; what kind of money would be used there; and what you might expect to find in the way of customs and landscape."

3. On individual sheets of paper or cardboard, the teacher can affix a cartoon clipped from the daily newspaper. (More mature children may be able to interpret a political cartoon; younger children may need a more humorous type.) The students would be asked what message the drawing is trying to convey, whom the characters are supposed to represent (as in a political caricature), why it is humorous, and whether they agree with the idea expressed by the artist.

4. The teacher can contrive a hypothetical table of contents or choose an actual table of contents from a content-area book and compile a series of questions asking the student to specify on what page he might expect to find certain information (information such as how the speed of wind is measured). A similar set of questions can be drawn up for an index.

5. From a supply of advertisements clipped from newspapers and magazines, the teacher can choose one advertisement to mount on a 9x12 sheet of poster board. On the same board can be listed several questions involving critical reading, such as "What is there in this ad that suggests that this brand is better than another?" "What associations are pictured with the product to make it more appealing?" "What statements are made that could well be false or misleading or a matter of opinion?" Questions should be so worded as to relate directly to the piece of advertising at hand.

6. A newspaper or magazine review of a television program, book, stage show, or movie may serve as the basis for questions involving critical reading. (A typical question might be "Would you want to see this movie after reading this review? Why?") This activity will be most meaningful to the student who has seen the dramatic presentation or read the book. It might also motivate a student to read the book if he has not done so.

7. The student can be given a road map covering a particular state or region and told to plot a trip from one specified place to another. He can be asked to compute the distance, to find the roads most suitable to take, to list the intervening towns having the same population as the one in which he lives, and so forth.

8. The student can be directed to choose a familiar nursery rhyme or fairy tale and rewrite it with modern characters and setting, using colloquial language.

9. The teacher can make up a list of ten arithmetic problems each of which lacks necessary information or contains extraneous information not needed to solve the problem. The student is to indicate what is missing or superfluous.

10. The student can be instructed to choose a library book written at the level of the primary or preschool child and then asked to read and evaluate it in terms of whether he thinks the story would appeal to a small child, whether the pictures are appealing and sufficient in number, whether a young child reading the book unaided might have trouble with certain words, whether the book is too long or not long enough, and so forth.

11. Directed to a reference book for factual information, the student might be asked to write a paragraph sketch about a famous person, without naming the person. The sketch could then either be posted or be read orally to the entire class so that the other students might individually or collectively attempt to guess the identity of the famous person from the given clues. (Of course, the student writing the sketch should be cautioned about offering a sufficient but not an excessive number of clues.)

12. On one or two notebook pages, the student might describe a famous event in history, throwing in some erroneous information (such as names of famous people not involved in the event) or inserting some occurrences out of sequence. The rest of the class might then try to determine what is wrong with the description. Reference books should be used for proof.

13. Many a problem situation can be created for the student in order to develop his reference skills. A typical problem might be this: "Imagine your mother is planning a birthday party for your six-year-old brother. She has asked you to be in charge of the games. Choose three or four games (using reference game books), write down the directions, and tell why you selected the ones you did, what equipment you will need, what plans you will have to make."

14. The student can be told to imagine that he has twenty dollars to spend on Christmas gifts for members of his family—the gifts to be selected from listings in a collection of mail-order catalogs. The student is to be asked to write out the order blanks, indicating such information as sizes, colors, code numbers, and postage fees.

15. After the student has examined certain sections in two or more content-area texts, he can be requested to write a short summary telling which book he thinks does the best job of providing information about the specified subject. The subjects can be "How to treat a snake bite," "What makes it rain?" "How do people in Germany earn a living?" and the like.

16. On a tagboard or cardboard, the teacher might clip two or more newspaper accounts dealing with the same incident. The student should then analyze how the same incident is reported differently and give his evaluation and explanation of the differences.

17. The student can be asked to make a list of ten words that do not follow the one-vowel rule (that is, the rule that the vowel between two consonants in a one-vowel word or accented syllable is usually short). This activity can be altered ad infinitum to take care of the various phonics rules.

18. The student can be instructed to make a list of ten or more general articles that have come to be known by one of their commercial names (such as cellophane, for transparent wrapping material in general). He can further be asked to investigate the nature of copyrights and patents and the part they play in the publicizing of products.

19. On the chalkboard or on ditto sheets, the teacher can print groups of sentences without capitalization or punctuation. The student is requested to copy the sentences, making the proper corrections.

20. The teacher can select two to six descriptive sentences from a story recently read and have the children write each sentence at the bottom of a sheet of drawing paper and draw a picture to illustrate the sentence.

21. Given a collection of mounted pictures, the child can be asked to write a descriptive sentence or two to identify or explain each picture.

22. The child can be directed to the vocabulary list in the back of a reader or content-area book and be asked to make a list of words that follow a particular rule of syllabication (such as the syllable rule that words divide between two consonants standing between two vowels), as well as a list of words that *do not* follow a particular rule. Phonics as well as syllabication rules can be used.

23. A short story from a magazine can be cut up into parts, which can be mounted on separate tagboards. The child is asked to number the parts in proper order. This activity can also be designed for oral reading by assigning different parts to different children (giving each child a chance first to read his part silently).

24. The itemized directions for making something (such as an article of prepared food or a piece of handicraft) can be separated and then printed separately

on index cards (or printed out of sequence on one card). The student is asked to rearrange (or number) the directions in proper sequence.

25. From a collection of short stories clipped from magazines (for younger children, from magazines such as *Highlights* or *Humpty Dumpty*) the teacher can choose one from which to excise the ending or final portion. Without seeing this final portion, the child writes his own ending and later compares his with the original.

26. For each word in a list provided by the teacher, the child is asked to name a word that either (1) "means the opposite" (an antonym), (2) "sounds the same" (a homonym), (3) "means the same" (a synonym), or (4) "spells the same except for a different beginning or ending letter." Younger children can be asked merely to write the word given by the teacher and then *draw* a picture of an object representing the other word called for (a picture of a *girl* as the antonym for *boy;* a picture of the *sea* as a homonym for *see;* a picture of a *nest* for a word spelled like *rest* except for the difference in beginning letters).

27. Among the many ongoing projects which the teacher can supervise and in which all students can participate is the compiling of booklets on various subjects (for example, a phonics booklet or a booklet on transportation). To illustrate these booklets, each child can be asked to clip pictures from a magazine or draw his own pictures to be pasted on specified pages. (A booklet of the seasons, might be illustrated with pictures of activities common during certain seasons.)

28. Each student can be asked to rearrange a single list of some twenty-five words in separate columns representing predesignated categories, such as "Things We Eat," "Things We Wear," "Things We Play With."

29. After having read a certain story, a child can be asked to make a cardboard figure of one of the story's characters. This figure is then set up in a shoe box (a "peep box") for other students to look at and evaluate; perhaps the other students might even be asked to guess the identity of the character portrayed and the story from which it came.

30. From among the stories already read by the entire class, a child can be asked to choose one to illustrate with his own drawing. The other students are then asked to view the completed drawing and guess the name of the story being depicted.

31. From various magazines and newspapers, the teacher can collect an assortment of illustrations presenting scenes that the students will find wildly comic, extravagant, or fanciful—that is, scenes from old silent movies, tableaus from the Victorian era, some advertisements of current movies, and the like. (*MAD* magazine is often a good source for such material.) These illustrations can be distributed one to a student, who can be asked to invent a caption that is humorous because of its inappropriateness or incongruity.

32. The teacher can provide the students with magazines or pamphlets containing mail-order advertisements for free materials (the Bantam paperback *1001 Valuable Things You Can Get Free,* edited by Mort Weisinger, is one useful source booklet). Each student can be asked to select one item from these sources and compose a letter requesting it from the manufacturer or distributor.

33. The student can be asked to write a letter, story, or essay, using rebus pictures in place of the nouns or verbs.

34. From a book containing puzzles, games, riddles, or tricks, the student can be asked to choose one activity and be prepared to demonstrate it or introduce it to the class.

35. The student can be asked to take a joke, a funny story, or a humorous incident drawn from an experience at school or home or from a book and to portray the incident in a comic-strip format.

36. Postage stamps commemorating famous people or events can be mounted on index cards along with questions designed to arouse interest and direct research. Typical questions could be "When did this person live?" "Why is he famous?" "What people took part in this event?" "What made this event important?"

37. The student can be asked to use ideas from a specific passage he has read to write a ten-word telegram, then a twenty-five-word night letter, and finally a personal letter. Newspaper and magazine articles as well as content-area material can be used as sources for this activity. *Main idea*

38. At the top of a sheet of paper, the teacher can print two letters of the alphabet with a space between them (E_____T). The child is instructed to write as many words as he can that begin and end with these letters (ea*t*, even*t*, eigh*t*, earnes*t*, *e*lephan*t*)—one point being awarded the child for each letter he adds. If two or more students are engaged in this activity, competitive scores can be kept and the results compared.

39. On the chalkboard or on ditto sheets can be printed lists of spelling words with their letters scrambled (as in anagrams), and opposite each scrambled word can be printed a synonym or brief definition. The student's task is to try to unscramble the words.

40. The teacher can provide a list of definitions as clues to the spelling of a word that he is "thinking about." The students are asked to consult a spelling list to select the proper word to fit the description. An example might be the following: "Think of a word that means the opposite of dull. This word has a long vowel. Drop the first letter of this word and it will mean 'correct.'" (Answer: *bright.*)

41. With grocery or supermarket advertisements clipped from the newspa-

per, the children can be instructed to make up a shopping list of food items and total the prices. Or, similarly, the teacher can prescribe a family's dinner menu and have the children compute the total cost of the food items that need to be purchased. Depending on the students' grade level, the problems might call for some involved computations—such as the price of three pounds of beef roast at seventy-nine cents a pound, or the price of one can of tomatoes at three cans for eighty cents.

42. The teacher can make up or obtain menus from restaurants and have the children decide what items they would choose, how much the total dinner would cost, and, in paying the check, how much change they would get back from a given bill of currency. If the ability level warrants, the 15 percent tip (and the state sales tax, if there is one) might be added.

43. Provided with a telephone book, the student can be asked to seek answers to such questions as "On what page will you find George St. John's telephone number?" "How many candy stores are listed in the yellow pages?" What is the number of the local post office?" "Under what heading in the yellow section do you look to find someone who can repair your family's toaster?"

44. Given the classified or want-ad section of a newspaper, the student can be asked a series of questions that call either for interpreting individual ads or for analyzing that newspaper's particular system of ad categories or classifications. Typical questions might be "How many ads are seeking employment for a woman?" "Under what heading do you find information about house trailers for sale?" "What is the rate for placing ads in this paper?" "What kinds of pets are offered for sale?"

45. The student can be asked to take a newspaper or magazine article or a page from an old workbook and delete from each sentence what he feels is any nonessential word or words.

46. A student can choose any story known to most class members and be asked to draw a picture of one incident for the class to identify. A similar activity would involve asking the student to write a paragraph about an incident in a story, although he should be cautioned not to reveal so much information that the class could immediately identify the story being described.

Books and Pamphlets on Independent Activities

CIOTTI, RITA, and KRAVITZ, IDA. *Independent Reading Activities*. Philadelphia: Great Cities Improvement Program, Philadelphia Board of Education.

DARROW, HELEN F., and ALLEN, R. VAN. *Independent Activities for Creative Learning*. New York: Bureau of Publications, Teachers College, Columbia Univ., 1961.

ECKGREN, BETTY LOIS, and FISHEL, VIVIAN. *500 Live Ideas for the Grade Teacher*. New York: Harper & Row, 1952.

HAIN, MARGARET, and FREEMAN, SARA. *Seatwork for Primary Grades.* San Francisco: Fearon, 1961.

A Handbook of Independent Activities to Promote Creativity in Children. San Diego, Calif.: Superintendent of Schools, Department of Education, San Diego County, October 1959.

HERR, SELMA E. *Learning Activities for Reading.* Dubuque, Iowa: William C. Brown, 1961.

Independent Activities for First Grade. Minneapolis: Department of Elementary Education, Minneapolis Public Schools, 1956.

Independent Activities for Primary Grades. (Teaching Staff Bulletin FC-4.) Warren, Ohio: Warren Public Schools, September 1956.

JOLLISON, MARION. *It's Fun to Learn.* New York: Hart, 1958.

Knoxville City Schools. *The Other Children: A Seatwork Activities Bulletin.* New York: Harper & Row, 1960.

Let's Play a Game. (Circular No. 404.) Boston: Ginn, January 1964.

McCULLOUGH, CONSTANCE M. "Independent Reading Activities," *Contributions in Reading,* No. 10. Boston: Ginn.

PLATTS, MARY E.; SISTER ROSE MARGUERITE; and SHUMAKER, ESTHER. *Spice: Suggested Activities to Motivate the Teaching of the Language Arts in the Elementary Schools.* Benton Harbor, Mich.: Educational Service, 1960.

A Potpourri of Reading Recipes. Wilmington, Del.: Elementary Division, Wilmington Public Schools, 1960.

Reading Activities for Non-Reciting Groups in the Elementary Grades. (Curriculum Bulletin No. 5.) Omaha: Department of Curriculum, Omaha Public Schools, September 1951.

Reading Games and Activities for the Middle Grades. (Circular No. 156.) Boston: Ginn, April 1964.

Resource Bulletin for Independent Work Activities. Ridgewood, N.J.: Ridgewood Public Schools, November 1953.

RUSSELL, DAVID H., and KARP, ETTA E. *Reading Aids Through the Grades.* New York: Bureau of Publications, Teachers College, Columbia Univ., 1961.

Such Interesting Things to Do! Independent Activities in the Language Arts for Grades One and Two. Chicago: Scott, Foresman, 1963.

TAIT, GEORGE E. (ed.) *100 Types of Primary Seatwork: A Handbook to Assist Teachers in the Development of Profitable, Interesting Grade One Seatwork.* Regina, Ont.: School Aids and Textbook Publishing Co., 1949.

WAGNER, GUY W., and HOSIER, MAX. *Reading Games: Strengthening Reading Skills with Instructional Games.* (Grade Teacher Publication.) Darien, Conn.: Educational Publishing Corp., 1960.

WAGNER, GUY W.; HOSIER, MAX; and BLACKMAN, MILDRED. *Listening Games: Building Listening Skills with Instructional Games.* (Grade Teacher Publication.) Darien, Conn.: Teachers Publishing Co., 1962.

BIBLIOGRAPHIES

Books and Materials for Teachers of Reading

NOTE: This represents a basic list. It is followed by a second bibliography for the reading consultant. Although there is a certain amount of overlapping, the second bibliography contains more specialized and, in some cases, more advanced material of particular interest to the consultant.

ALLEN, R. VAN, and LEE, DORRIS MAY. *Learning to Read Through Experience*. New York: Appleton-Century-Crofts, 1963.

ALTICK, RICHARD D. *Preface to Critical Reading*. 4th ed. New York: Holt, Rinehart & Winston, 1960.

ARBUTHNOT, MAY H. *Children and Books*. 3d ed. Chicago: Scott, Foresman, 1964.

BAMMAN, HENRY A.; HOGAN, URSULA; and GREENE, CHARLES E. *Reading Instruction in the Secondary School*. New York: McKay, 1961.

BARBE, WALTER B. *Educator's Guide to Personalized Reading Instruction*. Englewood Cliffs, N.J.: Prentice-Hall, 1961.

BETTS, EMMETT A. *Foundations of Reading Instruction*. New York: American Book, 1957.

BOND, GUY L., and TINKER, MILES A. *Reading Difficulties: Their Diagnosis and Correction*. New York: Appleton-Century-Crofts, 1957.

BOND, GUY L., and WAGNER, EVA B. *Teaching the Child to Read*. 3d. ed. New York: Macmillan, 1960.

BOTEL, MORTON. *How to Teach Reading*. Chicago: Follett, 1962.

BULLOCK, HARRISON. *Helping the "Non-Reading" Pupil in the Secondary School*. New York: Bureau of Publications, Teachers College, Columbia Univ., 1956.

BURTON, WILLIAM H., and others. *Reading in Child Development*. New York: Bobbs-Merrill, 1956.

CARTER, HOMER L. J., and McGINNIS, DOROTHY J. *Teaching Individuals to Read*. Boston: Heath, 1962.

DAWSON, MILDRED A., and BAMMAN, HENRY A. *Fundamentals of Basic Reading Instruction*. 2d ed. New York: McKay, 1963.

DEBOER, JOHN J., and DALLMANN, MARTHA. *The Teaching of Reading*. New York: Holt, Rinehart & Winston, 1964.

DECHANT, EMERALD V. *Improving the Teaching of Reading*. Englewood Cliffs, N.J.: Prentice-Hall, 1963.

DOLCH, EDWARD W. *Teaching Primary Reading*. Champaign, Ill.: Garrard, 1960.

DURRELL, DONALD D. *Improving Reading Instruction*. New York: Harcourt, Brace & World, 1956.

GANS, ROMA. *Common Sense in Teaching Reading*. Indianapolis: Bobbs-Merrill, 1963.

GATES, ARTHUR I. *The Improvement of Reading.* 3d ed. New York: Macmillan, 1947

GRAY, LILLIAN. *Teaching Children to Read.* 3d ed. New York: Ronald Press, 1963.

GRAY, WILLIAM S. *On Their Own in Reading.* Rev. ed. Chicago: Scott, Foresman, 1960.

HARRIS, ALBERT J. *Effective Teaching of Reading.* New York: McKay, 1962.

————. *How to Increase Reading Ability.* 4th ed. New York: McKay, 1961.

———— (ed.). *Readings on Reading Instruction.* New York: McKay, 1963.

HEILMAN, ARTHUR W. *Phonics in Proper Perspective.* Columbus, Ohio: Merrill, 1964.

————. *Principles and Practices of Teaching Reading.* Columbus, Ohio: Merrill, 1961.

HILDRETH, GERTRUDE H. *Teaching Reading: A Guide to Basic Principles and Modern Practices.* New York: Holt, Rinehart & Winston, 1958.

HUCK, CHARLOTTE S., and YOUNG, DORIS A. *Children's Literature in the Elementary School.* New York: Holt, Rinehart & Winston, 1961.

International Reading Association. *College-Adult Reading Instruction.* ("Perspectives in Reading," No. 1.) Newark, Del.: the Association, 1964.

KARLIN, ROBERT. *Teaching Reading in the High School.* Indianapolis: Bobbs-Merrill, 1963.

KOTTMEYER, WILLIAM. *Teacher's Guide for Remedial Reading.* St. Louis: Webster Div., McGraw-Hill, 1959.

MCKEE, PAUL. *The Teaching of Reading in the Elementary School.* Boston: Houghton Mifflin, 1948.

MCKIM, MARGARET G. *Guiding Growth in Reading in the Modern Elementary School.* 2d ed. New York: Macmillan, 1963.

National Society for the Study of Education. *Development in and Through Reading.* (60th Yearbook, Part 1.) Chicago: Univ. of Chicago Press, 1961.

————. *Reading in the Elementary School.* (48th Yearbook, Part 2.) Chicago: Univ. of Chicago Press, 1949.

————. *Reading in the High School and College.* (47th Yearbook, Part 2.) Chicago: Univ. of Chicago Press, 1948.

ROBINSON, FRANCIS P. *Effective Study.* Rev. ed. New York: Harper & Row, 1961.

ROBINSON, HELEN M. *Why Pupils Fail in Reading.* Chicago: Univ. of Chicago Press, 1946.

RUSSELL, DAVID H. *Children Learn to Read.* 2d ed. Boston: Ginn, 1961.

SHEPHERD, DAVID L. *Effective Reading in Science: A Handbook for Secondary Teachers.* New York: Harper & Row, 1960.

————. *Effective Reading in the Social Studies: A Handbook for Secondary Teachers.* New York: Harper & Row, 1960.

SMITH, NILA BANTON. *Reading Instruction for Today's Children.* Englewood Cliffs, N.J.: Prentice-Hall, 1963.

SPACHE, GEORGE D. *Reading in the Elementary School.* Boston: Allyn & Bacon, 1964.

————. *Toward Better Reading.* Champaign, Ill.: Garrard, 1963.

STRANG, RUTH. *Diagnostic Teaching of Reading.* New York: McGraw-Hill, 1964.

———— and BRACKEN, DOROTHY K. *Making Better Readers.* Boston: Heath, 1957.

———— and LINDQUIST, DONALD M. *The Administrator and the Improvement of Reading.* New York: Appleton-Century-Crofts, 1960.

———— McCULLOUGH, CONSTANCE M., and TRAXLER, ARTHUR. *The Improvement of Reading.* 3d ed. New York: McGraw-Hill, 1961.

TINKER, MILES A., and McCULLOUGH, CONSTANCE M. *Teaching Elementary Reading.* 2d ed. New York: Appleton-Century-Crofts, 1961.

UMANS, SHELLEY. *New Trends in Reading Instruction.* New York: Bureau of Publications, Teachers College, Columbia Univ., 1963.

VEATCH, JEANETTE. *Individualizing Your Reading Program.* New York: Putnam, 1959.

WITTY, PAUL. *Reading in Modern Education.* Boston: Heath, 1949.

YOAKAM, GERALD A. *Basal Reading Instruction.* New York: McGraw-Hill, 1955.

CONFERENCE PROCEEDINGS

International Reading Association Conference Proceedings. New York: Scholastic Magazines, 1956– .

Claremont College Reading Conference Yearbook. Claremont, Calif.: Claremont College Curriculum Library, 1945 (v. 10)– .

Lehigh University Reading Conference Proceedings. Bethlehem, Pa.: the University, 1961– .

National Reading Conference for Colleges and Adults Yearbook. Fort Worth: Texas Christian Univ. Press. 1958 (v. 7)– . (A continuation of the *Southwest Reading Conference for Colleges and Universities Yearbook.*)

National Reading Conference Yearbook. Milwaukee: Reading Center, Marquette Univ., 1952– .

Proceedings of the Conference on Reading. Newark: Univ. of Delaware, 1950– .

Proceedings of the Annual Conference on Reading at the University of Chicago. Chicago: Univ. of Chicago Press, 1939– .

Reading Conference, University of South Carolina. *Addresses and Discussions.* Columbia: School of Education, the University, 1960- .

Southwest Reading Conference for Colleges and Universities Yearbook. Fort Worth: Texas Christian Univ. Press, 1953–57. (Superseded by the *National Reading Conference for Colleges and Adults Yearbook.*)

University of Pittsburgh Annual Conference on Reading. Pittsburgh: the University, 1945– .

PAMPHLETS AND BULLETINS

DARROW, HELEN F., and HOWES, VIRGIL M. *Approaches to Individualized Reading.* New York: Appleton-Century-Crofts, 1960.

DEIGHTON, LEE C. *Vocabulary Development in the Classroom.* New York: Bureau of Publications, Teachers College, Columbia Univ., 1959.

DURKIN, DOLORES. *Phonics and the Teaching of Reading.* New York: Bureau of Publications, Teachers College, Columbia Univ., 1962.

FAY, LEO, and others. *Improving Reading in the Elementary Social Studies.* (Bulletin No. 33.) Washington: National Council for the Social Studies, 1961.

International Reading Association. *Children, Books and Reading.* ("Perspectives in Reading," No. 3.) Newark, Del.: the Association, 1964.

————. *Sources of Good Books for Poor Readers,* ed. GEORGE D. SPACHE. Newark, Del.: the Association, 1964. Annotated bibliography.

JEWETT, ARNO, and others. *Improving English Skills of Culturally Different Youth in Large Cities.* (Bulletin No. 5.) Washington: Office of Education, 1964.

Kansas University, School of Education. *Kansas Studies in Education,* Vol. 10: *Teaching Reading in the High School.* Lawrence: the University, 1960.

KLARE, GEORGE R. *The Measurement of Reliability.* Ames: Iowa State Univ. Press, 1963.

LAZAR, MAY (ed.). *A Practical Guide to Individualized Reading.* (Bureau of Education Research Publication No. 40.) New York: Board of Education, 1960.

MEEKER, ALICE M. *Teaching Beginners to Read.* New York: Holt, Rinehart & Winston, 1958.

Metropolitan School Study Council. *Five Steps to Reading Success in Science, Social Studies, and Mathematics.* Rev. ed. New York: Metropolitan School Study Council, Teachers College, Columbia Univ., 1960.

MIEL, ALICE (ed.). *Individualizing Reading Practices.* (Practical Suggestions for Teachers No. 14.) New York: Bureau of Publications, Teachers College, Columbia Univ., 1958.

PRESTON, RALPH C., and others. *Guiding the Social Studies Reading of High School Students.* (Bulletin No. 34.) Washington: National Council for the Social Studies, 1963.

SOCHOR, E. ELONA, and others. *Critical Reading: An Introduction.* (A bulletin of the National Conference on Research in English, reprinted from *Elementary English.*) Champaign, Ill.: National Council of Teachers of English, 1959.

JOURNALS

Elementary English. National Council of Teachers of English, 508 S. 6th St., Champaign, Ill. 61821. 1 year, $5.

The Elementary School Journal. The University of Chicago Press, 5750 S. Ellis Ave., Chicago, Ill. 60637. 1 year, $4.50; 2 years, $8.50; 3 years, $12.

The English Journal. National Council of Teachers of English, 508 S. 6th St., Champaign, Ill. 61821. 1 year, $5.

Journal of Reading. International Reading Association, Box 119, Newark, Del. 19711. 1 year, $4.50; for IRA members, $4.

The Journal of Reading Specialists. College Reading Association, Reading Clinic, Lehigh University, Bethlehem, Pa. 18015. 1 year, $4.

Reading in High School. Box 75, College Sta., Pullman, Wash. 99163. 1 year, $3.50; for college students, $2.

The Reading Teacher. International Reading Association, Box 119, Newark, Del. 19711. 1 year, $4.50; for IRA members, $4.

Selected Books and Materials for the Reading Consultant

NOTE: Those titles marked with an asterisk have been cited in the preceding professional library list and are listed again for the convenience of the consultant.

*ALTICK, RICHARD D. *Preface to Critical Reading.* 4th ed. New York: Holt, Rinehart & Winston, 1960.

AUSTIN, MARY C.; BUSH, CLIFFORD L.; and HUEBNER, MILDRED H. *Reading Evaluation.* New York: Ronald Press, 1961.

Austin, Mary C.; Morrison, Coleman; and others. *The First R: The Harvard Report on Reading in Elementary Schools.* New York: Macmillan, 1963.

Austin, Mary C., and others. *The Torch Lighters: Tomorrow's Teachers of Reading.* Cambridge, Mass.: Harvard Univ. Press, 1961.

Blair, Glenn. *Diagnostic and Remedial Teaching.* Rev. ed. New York: Macmillan, 1956.

*Bond, Guy L., and Tinker, Miles A. *Reading Difficulties: Their Diagnosis and Correction.* New York: Appleton-Century-Crofts, 1957.

*Bond, Guy L., and Wagner, Eva B. *Teaching the Child to Read.* 3d ed. New York: Macmillan, 1960.

*Botel, Morton. *How to Teach Reading.* Chicago: Follett, 1962.

*Bullock, Harrison. *Helping the "Non-Reading" Pupil in the Secondary School.* New York: Bureau of Publications, Teachers College, Columbia Univ., 1956.

Cutts, Warren G. *Modern Reading Instruction.* Washington: Center for Applied Research in Education, 1964.

*Dechant, Emerald V. *Improving the Teaching of Reading.* Englewood Cliffs, N.J.: Prentice-Hall, 1963.

Delacato, Carl. *The Diagnosis and Treatment of Speech and Reading Problems.* Springfield, Ill.: Charles C. Thomas, 1963.

Dever, Kathryn Imogene. *Positions in the Field of Reading.* New York: Bureau of Publications, Teachers College, Columbia Univ., 1956.

Ephron, Beulah K. *Emotional Difficulties in Reading.* New York: Julian Press, 1953.

Fernald, Grace M. *Remedial Techniques in Basic School Subjects.* New York: McGraw-Hill, 1943.

*Gray, William S. *On Their Own in Reading.* Rev. ed. Chicago: Scott, Foresman, 1960.

*Harris, Albert J. *How to Increase Reading Ability.* 4th ed. New York: McKay, 1961.

Hayakawa, Samuel I. *Language in Thought and Action.* Rev. ed. New York: Harcourt, Brace & World, 1962.

Keyes, Kenneth S. *How to Develop Your Thinking Ability.* New York: McGraw-Hill, 1950.

Kolsom, Clifford J., and Cleland, Donald L. *Clinical Aspects of Remedial Reading.* Springfield, Ill.: Charles C. Thomas, 1963.

*Kottmeyer, William. *Teacher's Guide for Remedial Reading.* St. Louis: Webster Div., McGraw-Hill, 1959.

McCallister, James M. *Remedial and Corrective Instruction in Reading.* New York: Appleton-Century, 1936.

Money, John (ed.). *Reading Disability: Progress and Research Needs in Dyslexia.* Baltimore: Johns Hopkins Press, 1962.

*National Society for the Study of Education. *Development in and Through Reading.* (60th Yearbook, Part 1.) Chicago: Univ. of Chicago Press, 1961.

*———. *Reading in the Elementary School.* (48th Yearbook, Part 2.) Chicago: Univ. of Chicago Press, 1949.

*———. *Reading in the High School and College.* (47th Yearbook, Part 2.) Chicago: Univ. of Chicago Press, 1948.

NEWTON, J. ROY. *Reading in Your School.* New York: McGraw-Hill, 1960.

POLLACK, MYRON F. W., and PIERKARZ, JOSEPHINE. *Reading Problems and Problem Readers.* New York: McKay, 1963.

*ROBINSON, FRANCIS P. *Effective Study.* Rev. ed. New York: Harper & Row, 1961.

ROBINSON, HELEN M. (ed.). *Clinical Studies in Reading II.* (Supplementary Educational Monographs No. 68.) Chicago: Univ. of Chicago Press, 1953.

*————. *Why Pupils Fail in Reading.* Chicago: Univ. of Chicago Press, 1946.

ROSWELL, FLORENCE, and NATCHEZ, GLADYS. *Reading Disability: Diagnosis and Treatment.* New York: Basic Books, 1963.

SCHONELL, FRED J. *The Psychology and Teaching of Reading.* 2d ed. Edinburgh: Oliver & Boyd, 1946.

*SHEPHERD, DAVID L. *Effective Reading in Science: A Handbook for Secondary Teachers.* New York: Harper & Row, 1960.

*————. *Effective Reading in the Social Studies: A Handbook for Secondary Teachers.* New York: Harper & Row, 1960.

SMITH, HENRY P., and DECHANT, EMERALD V. *Psychology in Teaching Reading.* Englewood Cliffs, N.J.: Prentice-Hall, 1961.

*SPACHE, GEORGE D. *Toward Better Reading.* Champaign, Ill.: Garrard, 1963.

Staff of the Reading Clinics of the University of Chicago. *Clinical Studies in Reading I.* (Supplementary Educational Monographs No. 77.) Chicago: Univ. of Chicago Press, 1949.

*STRANG, RUTH. *Diagnostic Teaching of Reading.* New York: McGraw-Hill, 1964.

*———— and BRACKEN, DOROTHY K. *Making Better Readers.* Boston: Heath, 1957.

*———— McCULLOUGH, CONSTANCE M., and TRAXLER, ARTHUR. *The Improvement of Reading.* 3d ed. New York: McGraw-Hill, 1961.

*UMANS, SHELLEY. *New Trends in Reading Instruction.* New York: Bureau of Publications, Teachers College, Columbia Univ., 1963.

VERNON, MAGDALEN D. *Backwardness in Reading: A Study of Its Origin and Nature.* New York: Cambridge Univ. Press, 1957.

WOOLF, MAURICE D., and WOOLF, JEANNE A. *Remedial Reading: Teaching Treatment.* New York: McGraw-Hill, 1957.

PAMPHLETS AND BULLETINS

CUTTS, WARREN G. *Research in Reading for the Middle Grades.* (Bulletin No. 31.) Washington: Office of Education, 1963.

———— (ed.) *Teaching Young Children to Read.* (Bulletin No. 19.) Washington: Office of Education, 1964.

*DEIGHTON, LEE C. *Vocabulary Development in the Classroom.* New York: Bureau of Publications, Teachers College, Columbia Univ., 1959.

*DURKIN, DOLORES. *Phonics and the Teaching of Reading.* New York: Bureau of Publications, Teachers College, Columbia Univ., 1962.

FAY, LEO C. *Improving the Teaching of Reading by Teacher Experimentation.* (Bulletin of the School of Education, Indiana University, Vol. 34, No. 5.) Bloomington: Division of Research and Field Services, the University, 1958.

————. *Reading in the High School.* ("What Research Says to the Teacher," Bulletin No. 11.) Washington: National Education Assn., 1956.

*———— and others. *Improving Reading in the Elementary Social Studies.* (Bulletin No. 33.) Washington: National Council for the Social Studies, 1961.

*International Reading Association. *Children, Books and Reading.* ("Perspectives in Reading," No. 3.) Newark, Del.: the Association, 1964.

*————. *Individualized Reading,* ed. HARRY SARTAIN. Newark, Del.: the Association, 1964. Annotated bibliography.

*————. *Providing Clinical Services in Reading,* ed. ROY A. KRESS and MARJORIE S. JOHNSON. Newark, Del.: the Association, 1964. Annotated bibliography.

*————. *Reading and the Kindergarten,* ed. DOLORES DURKIN. Newark, Del.: the Association, 1964. Annotated bibliography.

*————. *Reading in the Content Fields,* ed. LEO FAY. Newark, Del.: the Association, 1964. Annotated bibliography.

*————. *Reading Instruction in Secondary Schools.* ("Perspectives in Reading." No. 2.) Newark, Del.: the Association, 1964.

*————. *Sources of Good Books for Poor Readers,* ed. GEORGE D. SPACHE. Newark, Del.: the Association, 1964. Annotated bibliography.

JEWETT, ARNO (ed.). *Improving Reading in the Junior High School.* (Office of Education Bulletin No. 10.) Washington: Government Printing Office, 1957.

*———— and others. *Improving English Skills of Culturally Different Youth in Large Cities.* (Bulletin No. 5.) Washington: Office of Education, 1964.

*Kansas University, School of Education. *Kansas Studies in Education,* Vol. 10: *Teaching Reading in the High School.* Lawrence: the University, 1960.

Learning to Read: A Report of a Conference of Reading Experts. Princeton, N.J.: Educational Testing Service, 1962.

*Metropolitan School Study Council. *Five Steps to Reading Success in Science, Social Studies, and Mathematics.* Rev. ed. New York: Metropolitan School Study Council, Teachers College, Columbia Univ., 1960.

*PRESTON, RALPH C., and others. *Guiding the Social Studies Reading of High School Students.* (Bulletin No. 34.) Washington: National Council for the Social Studies, 1963.

*SOCHOR, E. ELONA, and others. *Critical Reading: An Introduction.* (A bulletin of the National Conference on Research in English, reprinted from *Elementary English.*) Champaign, Ill.: National Council of Teachers of English, 1959.

South Penn School Study Council Reading Committee (HELEN HUUS, consultant). *A Handbook for Developmental Reading.* Danville, Ill.: Interstate Printers & Publishers, 1961.

Selected Books and Materials on Reading for Parents

American Book Company, Reading Workshop. *Are Your Children Ready to Read?* New York: American Book, 1948.

ANDERSON, A. HELEN. *There's More to Reading than Meets the Eye.* Denver: Denver Public Schools, Division of Instructional Services, 1957.

ARTLEY, A. STERL. *Your Child Learns to Read.* Chicago: Scott, Foresman, 1953.

BOND, GUY L., and WAGNER, EVA B. *Child Growth in Reading.* Chicago: Lyons & Carnahan, 1955.

CASEY, SALLY L. *Ways You Can Help Your Child with Reading.* New York: Harper & Row, 1950.

CAVANAH, FRANCES (ed.). *Family Reading Festival.* Englewood Cliffs, N.J.: Prentice-Hall, 1958.

Chicago Public Schools. *Reading in the Chicago Public Schools.* Chicago: Chicago Public Schools, 1955.

COX, MARY ALINE. *Teach Your Child to Read: A Book for Parents.* 2d ed. New York: Exposition Press, 1953.

Detroit Public Schools. *A Guide to Instruction in the Language Arts: Early-Elementary Grades and Annex Volume.* Detroit: Board of Education of the City of Detroit, 1961. Available from Detroit Public Schools Information Service, 5057 Woodward Ave., Detroit, Mich. 48202.

DOLCH, EDWARD W. *Helping Your Child with Reading.* Champaign, Ill.: Garrard, 1956.

DUFF, ANNIS. *Longer Flight: A Family Grows Up with Books.* New York: Viking, 1955.

DUKER, SAM, and NALLY, THOMAS P. *The Truth About Your Child's Reading.* New York: Crown, 1956.

FENNER, PHYLLIS R. *The Proof of the Pudding: What Children Read.* New York: Day, 1957.

FRANK, JOSETTE. *Your Child's Reading Today.* Rev. ed. Garden City, N. Y.: Doubleday, 1960.

GANS, ROMA. *Reading Is Fun.* New York: Bureau of Publications, Teachers College, Columbia Univ., 1949.

GOLDENSON, ROBERT M. *Helping Your Child to Read Better.* New York: Thomas Y. Crowell, 1957.

HENDERSON, ELLEN C. *You Can Teach a Child That Reading Can Be Fun: A Guide for Parents and Teachers.* New York: Exposition Press, 1956.

HYMES, JAMES L., Jr. *Before the Child Reads.* New York: Harper & Row, 1958.

Inglewood Public Schools. *Good Ways of Helping Your Child in Reading.* Inglewood, Calif.: Board of Education, Inglewood Unified School District, 1957.

JUDD, ROMIE D. *Setting the Stage for Johnny to Read.* New York: Pageant Press, 1955.

LARRICK, NANCY. *A Parent's Guide to Children's Reading.* Garden City, N.Y.: Doubleday, 1958.

LEAF, MUNRO. *Reading Can Be Fun.* Philadelphia: Lippincott, 1953.

MacDOUGALL, URSULA C. *If Your Child Has Reading Difficulties.* New York: Dalton School, 1952.

McEARTHRON, MARGARET. *Your Child Can Learn to Read.* New York: Grosset & Dunlap, 1956.

McKEE, PAUL. *A Primer for Parents: How Your Child Learns to Read.* Boston: Houghton Mifflin, 1957.

MACKINTOSH, HELEN K. *How Children Learn to Read.* (Office of Education Bulletin No. 7.) Washington: Office of Education, 1952.

MERGENTINE, CHARLOTTE. *You and Your Child's Reading: A Practical Guide for Parents.* New York: Harcourt, Brace & World, 1963.

Metropolitan School Study Council. *Yes, We Teach Reading: A Primer for Parents on Their School's Reading Program.* New York: Metropolitan School Study Council, Teachers College, Columbia Univ., 1953.

MONROE, MARION. *Growing into Reading*. Chicago: Scott, Foresman, 1951.

Montclair Public Schools. *How Parents Can Help Their Children with Reading*. Montclair, N. J.: Division of Instruction and Guidance, Montclair Public Schools, 1952.

National Education Association, Department of Elementary School Principals, National School Public Relations Association and National Congress of Parents and Teachers. *Happy Journey: Preparing Your Child for School*. Washington: the Association, 1953.

National Education Association, Department of Elementary School Principals, National School Public Relations Association. *How to Help Your Child Learn: A Handbook for Parents of Children in Kindergarten Through Grade 6*. Washington: the Association, 1960.

————. *Janie Learns to Read: A Handbook for Parents Whose Child Will Soon Learn to Read*. Washington: the Association, 1956.

————. *Sailing into Reading: How Your Child Learns to Read in the Elementary School*. Washington: the Association, 1956.

New York State Education Department, Bureau of Elementary Curriculum Development. *The First "R," Reading*. Albany: New York Education Dept., 1955.

RASMUSSEN, MARGARET (ed.). *Reading*. (1956–57 Membership Service Bulletin No. 98.) Washington: Assn. for Childhood Education International, 1956.

The Reading Teacher, VII (April 1954). Entire issue.

STRANG, RUTH. *Helping Your Child Improve His Reading*. New York: Dutton, 1962.

————. *Helping Your Gifted Child*. New York: Dutton, 1960.

TOOZE, RUTH. *Your Children Want to Read: A Guide for Teachers and Parents*. Englewood Cliffs, N.J.: Prentice-Hall, 1957.

University of Delaware Reading Clinic. *Proceedings of the Annual Parent Conference on Reading,* Vol. I: *What Parents Can Do to Help Their Children in Reading,* ed. RUSSELL G. STAUFFER. Newark: Univ. of Delaware Reading Clinic, 1950.

VAN ATTA, FRIEDA A. *How to Help Your Child in Reading, Writing, and Arithmetic*. New York: Random House, 1959.

VAN ROEKEL, G. H. *Preparing Your Child for First Steps in Reading*. (Professional Series Bulletin No. 6) East Lansing: Bureau of Research and Service, School of Education, Michigan State Univ., 1955.

Vernal Public Schools. *Time to Read: Parents Can Help*. Vernal, Utah: Vernal Public Schools.

Warren Public Schools. *How Does Your Child Learn to Read?* Warren, Ohio: Warren City Schools, 1954.

WITTY, PAUL. *Helping Children Read Better*. (Better Living Booklet No. 501.) Chicago: Science Research Associates, 1950.

List of Educational Publishers

Allyn and Bacon, Inc., 150 Tremont St., Boston, Mass. 02111

American Book Co., 55 Fifth Ave., New York, N.Y. 10003

Appleton-Century-Crofts, affiliate of Meredith Publishing Co., 440 Park Ave. South, New York, N.Y. 10016.

The Bobbs-Merrill Co., Inc., subsidiary of Howard W. Sams & Co., Inc., 4300 W. 62d St., Indianapolis, Ind. 46206

Center for Applied Research in Education, division of Prentice-Hall, Inc., 70 Fifth Ave., New York, N.Y. 10011

Thomas Y. Crowell Co., 201 Park Ave. South, New York, N.Y. 10003

The Crowell-Collier Publishing Co., 640 Fifth Ave., New York, N.Y. 10019

Crown Publishers, Inc., 419 Park Ave. South, New York, N.Y. 10016

The John Day Co.: *see entry under "J."*

Doubleday & Company, Inc., Garden City, N.Y. 11530

E. P. Dutton & Co., Inc., 201 Park Ave. South, New York, N.Y 10003

Encyclopaedia Britannica Press, Inc., 425 N. Michigan Ave., Chicago, Ill. 60611

Follett Publishing Co., 1010 W. Washington Blvd., Chicago, Ill. 60607

Garrard Publishing Co., 1607 N. Market St., Champaign, Ill. 61821

Ginn & Company, Statler Bldg., Back Bay P.O. 191, Boston, Mass., 02117

Grosset & Dunlap, Inc., 1107 Broadway, New York, N.Y. 10010

Harcourt, Brace & World, Inc., 757 Third Ave., New York, N.Y. 10017

Harper & Row, Publishers, 49 E. 33d St., New York, N.Y. 10016

Harvard University Press, 79 Garden St., Cambridge, Mass. 02138

D. C. Heath & Company, 285 Columbus Ave., Boston, Mass. 02116

Holt, Rinehart & Winston, Inc., 383 Madison Ave., New York, N.Y. 10017

Houghton Mifflin Co., 2 Park St., Boston, Mass. 02107

The John Day Company, Inc., 62 W. 45th St., New York, N.Y. 10036

Julian Press, Inc., 119 Fifth Ave., New York, N.Y. 10003

Laidlaw Brothers, division of Doubleday & Co., Inc., Thatcher & Madison Sts., River Forest, Ill. 60305

J. B. Lippincott Co., E. Washington Sq., Philadelphia, Pa. 19105

Lyons & Carnahan, affiliate of Meredith Publishing Co., 407 E. 25th St., Chicago, Ill. 60616

McGraw-Hill Book Co., 330 W. 42d St., New York, N.Y. 10036

David McKay Co., Inc., 750 Third Ave., New York, N.Y. 10017

The Macmillan Company, division of the Crowell-Collier Publishing Co., 60 Fifth Ave., New York, N.Y. 10011

The Meredith Publishing Co., Textbook Division, 440 Park Ave. South, New York, N.Y. 10016

Charles E. Merrill Books, Inc., 1300 Alum Creek Dr., Columbus, Ohio 43216

Oliver and Boyd, Ltd., Tweeddale Court, 14 High St., Edinburgh 1, Scotland

Prentice-Hall, Inc., Englewood Cliffs, N.J. 07632

G. P. Putnam's Sons, 200 Madison Ave., New York, N.Y. 10016

Rand McNally & Co., 8255 Central Park Ave., Skokie, Ill. 60076

Random House, Inc., 457 Madison Ave., New York, N.Y. 10022

The Ronald Press Company, 15 E. 26th St., New York, N.Y. 10010

Scholastic Book Services, division of Scholastic Magazines, Inc., 50 W. 44th St., New York, N.Y. 10036

Science Research Associates, Inc., subsidiary of International Business Machines Corp., 259 E. Erie St., Chicago, Ill. 60611

Scott, Foresman & Company, 433 E. Erie St., Chicago, Ill. 60611

Charles Scribner's Sons, 597 Fifth Ave., New York, N.Y. 10017

Silver Burdett Company, subsidiary of Time Inc., Park Ave. & Columbia Rd., Morristown, N.J. 07960

The L. W. Singer Company, Inc., division of Random House, Inc., 249-259 W. Erie Blvd., Syracuse, N.Y. 13202

Teachers College, Bureau of Publications, Columbia University, 525 W. 120th St., New York, N.Y. 10027

Teachers Publishing Corp., Division of the Crowell-Collier Publishing Co., 23 Leroy Ave., Darien, Conn. 06820

The University of Chicago Press, 5750 Ellis Ave., Chicago, Ill. 60637

The University of Michigan Press, Ann Arbor, Mich. 48106

The Viking Press, 625 Madison Ave., New York, N.Y. 10022

Webster Publishing, division of McGraw-Hill Book Co., 1154 Reco Ave., St. Louis, Mo. 63126

AUDIO-VISUAL AIDS

NOTE: A number of these aids have not been reviewed. The purchase prices quoted are those current when this handbook went to press.

Vocabulary

Better Choice of Words. Coronet. Film. 1 reel, 11 min. Junior and senior high school. Color, $120; b & w, $60.

Build Your Vocabulary. Coronet. Film. 1 reel, 11 min. Junior and senior high school. Color, $120; b & w, $60.

Building Blocks of Vocabulary. Learning Through Seeing. 18 filmstrips. Senior high school through adult. $45.

Do Words Ever Fool You? Coronet. Film. 1 reel, 11 min. Intermediate. Color, $120; b & w, $60.

Fun with Words. Eye Gate House. Filmstrip. Primary, intermediate, junior high school. $4. (From *Fundamentals of Reading,* 9 colored filmstrips and teacher's manual, $30.)

Graded Word Phrases. Society for Visual Education. Filmstrips for each level, kindergarten through grade 6. $8 to $16.

Graded Word Phrases. Society for Visual Education. Filmstrips. Grades 7 through 12.

English Phrases	$2
Geography Phrases	$2
Health Phrases	$4
Mathematics Phrases	$2
Miscellaneous Phrases	$6
Science Phrases	$8
Social Studies Phrases	$8

How to Build a Bigger Vocabulary. Educational Recording Services. Record. Intermediate. $1.10.

How to Learn the Foundation Words. Educational Recording Services. Record. Primary. $1.10.

How to Make Your Vocabulary Grow. Educational Recording Services. Record. Intermediate. $1.10.

Improve Your Vocabulary. (Better Study Habits Series.) McGraw-Hill Elementary Films. Filmstrip. Elementary. $6.50.

Prefix Mastery. Learning Through Seeing. 12 filmstrips. Elementary through adult. $30.

Reading Improvement: Vocabulary Skills. Coronet. Film. 1 reel, 11 min. Junior and senior high school. Color, $120; b & w, $60.

Reading Series. Society for Visual Education. Separate filmstrips of words, word groups, familiar objects, for grades 1 through 6. Based on Dolch and Davis' basic vocabulary list of commonest nouns. $2.50 to $3.25.

Suffix Mastery. Learning Through Seeing. 12 filmstrips. Elementary through adult. $30.

Who Makes Words? Coronet. Film. 1 reel, 11 min. Elementary through senior high school. Color, $120; b & w, $60.

Word Building in Our Language. Coronet. Film. 1 reel, 11 min. Junior and senior high school. Color, $120; b & w, $60.

Word Mastery. Learning Through Seeing. 3 sets, 12 filmstrips each. Elementary through adult. $30 per set.

Word Study Series. McGraw-Hill. Filmstrips. Junior and senior high school. $7 each.
    Keys to Word Building
    Synonyms, Antonyms, Homonyms, Heteronyms
    Unusual Word Origins
    Words Derived from Latin and Greek
    Words Derived from Other Languages
    Word Meanings Change

Words: Their Origin, Use and Spelling. Society for Visual Education. 6 filmstrips. Grades 6 through 8. $5 each.

Comprehension

Better Reading. Encyclopaedia Britannica. Film. 13 min. Junior and senior high school. Color, $120; b & w, $60.

Better Study Habits Series: Improve Your Reading. McGraw-Hill Elementary Films. Filmstrip. Middle grades. $6.50.

Comprehension Skills. Perceptual Development Laboratories. Films and activities. 45 min. Junior and senior high school. Can be viewed only with Perceptoscope.

Orientation	$70
Outlining	$45
Paragraph Organization	$45
Paragraph Understanding	$45
Sentence Meaning	$70
Word Meaning Through Context	$45
Word Meaning Through Structure	$70

Developing Imagination. Coronet. Film. 1 reel, 11 min. Junior and senior high school. Color, $120; b & w, $60.

How Effective is Your Reading? Coronet. Film. 1 reel, 11 min. Junior and senior high school. Color, $120; b & w, $60.

How to Read a Book. Coronet. Film. 1 reel, 11 min. Junior and senior high school. Color, $120; b & w, $60.

How to Read a Narrative Poem. McGraw-Hill. Filmstrip. Junior and senior high school. $7.

How to Read a One-Act Play. McGraw-Hill. Filmstrip. Junior and senior high school. $7.

How to Read a Short Story. McGraw-Hill. Filmstrip. Junior and senior high school. $7.

How to Read an Historical Novel. McGraw-Hill. Filmstrip. Junior and senior high school. $7.

How to Read for Information. Educational Recording Services. Record. Intermediate. $1.10.

How to Read Newspapers. Coronet. Film. 1 reel, 11 min. Junior and senior high school. Color, $120; b & w, $60.

How to Read: To Understand, Evaluate, Use. Society for Visual Education. Filmstrip. 42 frames. Grades 7 through 12. $3.25.

Improve Your Reading. Coronet. Film. 1 reel, 11 min. Junior and senior high school. Color, $120; b & w, $50.

Let's Read Poetry. Bailey. Film. 1 reel, 10 min. Elementary and junior high school. Color, $100; b & w, $50.

Literature Appreciation: How to Read Essays. Coronet. Film. 1¼ reels, 13½ min. Junior and senior high school. Color, $150; b & w, $75.

Literature Appreciation: How to Read Novels. Coronet. Film. 1¼ reels, 13½ min. Junior and senior high school. Color, $150; black-and-white, $75.

Literature Appreciation: How to Read Plays. Coronet. Film. 1 reel, 11 min. Junior and senior high school. Color, $120; b & w, $60.

Literature Appreciation: How to Read Poetry. Coronet. Film. 1 reel, 11 min. Junior and senior high school. Color, $120; b & w, $60.

Literature Appreciation: Stories. Coronet. Film. 1¼ reels, 13½ min. Junior and senior high school. Color, $150; b & w, $75.

Making Sense With Outlines. Coronet. Film. 1 reel, 11 min. Intermediate. Color, $120; b & w, $60.

Pathway to Reading Series. C-B Educational. 5 films. Elementary through college. $350 for set.
  How to Read
  Was It Worth Reading?
  What Did You Read?
  What's In a Book?
  Why Read?

Poems Are Fun. Coronet. Film. 1 reel, 11 min. Intermediate. Color, $120; b & w, $60.

Reading a Cross-Section. Bel-Mort. Filmstrip. Elementary. $6.50.

Reading Effectively. Univ. of Iowa. Film. 10 min. High school. $45.

Reading Improvement: Comprehension Skills. Coronet. Film. 1 reel, 11 min. Junior and senior high school. Color, $120; b & w, $60.

Reading Improvement: Defining the Good Reader. Coronet. Film. 1 reel, 11 min. Junior and senior high school. Color, $120; b & w, $60.

Reading with a Purpose. Coronet. Film. 1 reel, 11 min. Intermediate. Color, $120; b & w, $60.

Ways to Improve Comprehension. Educational Recording Services. Record. Intermediate. $1.10.

Reading Rate

College Series of Iowa Reading Films. Univ. of Iowa. 15 films. 4-4½ min. $175.

High Speed Reading. Coronet. Film. 1 reel, 11 min. High school and college. Color, $120; b & w, $60.

Keys to Reading Series. C-B Educational Films. Elementary through college. 3 films, $225; 3 filmstrips, $15.
  Paragraphs
  Phrases
  Words

Phrase Reading Series. C-B Educational Films. $325 per set. (May be purchased individually.)

   Advanced Phrase Reading (6 films)

   Beginning Phrase Reading (sixth-grade level; 3 films; 6 min. each)

   Intermediate Phrase Reading (above sixth-grade level; 6 films)

   It's in the Phrase

Rapid Reading Process. Educational Devices. Film. 11½ min. Senior high school. $32.50.

Reading Improvement: Effective Speeds. Coronet. Film. Junior and senior high school. Color, $120; b & w, $60.

Revised High School Series of Films. Univ. of Iowa. 15 films. 3–4 min. each. $150.

Speeding Your Reading. Univ. of Iowa. Film. 10 min. Senior high school through adult. $50.

Study Skills

Better Study Habits Series: Improve Your Study Habits. McGraw-Hill Elementary Films. Filmstrips. Middle grades. $6.50.

Building an Outline. Coronet. Film. 1 reel, 11 min. Junior and senior high school. Color, $120; b & w, $60.

Building Work Habits Series. McGraw-Hill. 6 filmstrips and records. Middle grades. $60.

Do Better on Your Exams. Coronet. Film. 1 reel, 11 min. Junior and senior high school. Color, $120; b & w, $50.

Homework. Coronet. Film. 1 reel, 11 min. Junior and senior high school. Color, $120; b & w, $50.

How to Concentrate. Coronet. Film. 1 reel, 11 min. Junior and senior high school. Color, $120; b & w, $50.

How to Develop Interest. Coronet. Film. 1 reel, 11 min. Junior and senior high school. Color, $120; b & w, $60.

How to Judge Authorities. Coronet. Film. 1 reel, 11 min. Junior and senior high school. Color, $120; b & w, $50.

How to Judge Facts. Coronet. Film. 1 reel, 11 min. Junior and senior high school. Color, $120; b & w, $50.

How to Observe. Coronet. Film. 1 reel, 11 min. Junior and senior high school. Color, $120; b & w, $60.

How to Prepare a Class Report. Coronet. Film. 1 reel, 11 min. Junior and senior high school. Color, $120; b & w, $60.

How to Remember. Coronet. Film. 1 reel, 11 min. Junior and senior high school. Color, $120; b & w, $60.

How to Study. Coronet. Film. 1 reel, 11 min. Junior and senior high school. Color, $120; b & w, $50.

How to Succeed in School. McGraw-Hill. Film. 11 min. High school and college. $60.

How to Take a Test. Society for Visual Education. Filmstrip. 43 frames. Junior and senior high school. $5.

How to Take a Test. McGraw-Hill. Film. 10 min. Junior and senior high school. $60.

How to Think. Coronet. Film. 1½ reels, 13½ min. Junior and senior high school. Color, $120; b & w, $75.

How to Write Your Term Paper. Coronet. Film. 1 reel, 11 min. Junior and senior high school. Color, $120; b & w, $50.

How We Learn. Coronet. Film. 1 reel, 11 min. Junior and senior high school. Color, $120; b & w, $60.

Importance of Making Notes. Coronet. Film. 1 reel, 11 min. Junior high school through college. Color, $120; b & w, $60.

Improve Your Study Habits. Coronet. Film. 1 reel, 11 min. Color, $120; b & w, $60.

Keep Up with Your Studies. Coronet. Film. 1 reel, 11 min. Junior high school through college. Color, $120; b & w, $60.

Learning to Study. Jam Handy. Filmstrips. Junior and senior high school. $29.75 per set; $4.75 each.
    Getting Down to Work (34 frames)
    Giving a Book Report (29 frames)
    Reviewing (27 frames)
    Study Headquarters (33 frames)
    Taking Notes in Class (29 frames)
    Using a Textbook (26 frames)
    Writing a Research Paper (32 frames)

Preparing to Study. Society for Visual Education. Filmstrip. 39 frames. Junior and senior high school. $5.

Preparing Your Book Report. Coronet. Film. 1 reel, 11 min. Intermediate. Color, $120; b & w, $60.

Successful Scholarship. McGraw-Hill. Film. 11 min. High school and college. $65.

What to Ask, How and Where to Find the Answers. Society for Visual Education. Filmstrips. Junior and senior high school. $5 each.
    Part 1 (34 frames)
    Part 2 (26 frames)

Why Study? Society for Visual Education. Filmstrip. 39 frames. Junior and senior high school. $5.

Reference Aids

Dictionary Helps to Pronunciation. Educational Recording Services. Record. Intermediate. $1.10.

Discovering the Library. Coronet. Film. 1 reel, 11 min. Primary. Color, $120; b & w, $60.

Find the Information. Coronet. Film. 1 reel, 11 min. Intermediate. Color, $120; b & w, $60.

Getting the Most from the Library. Educational Recording Services. Record. Intermediate. $1.10.

How to Locate Words in a Dictionary. Educational Recording Services. Record. Age 9 and above. $1.10.

How to Use an Encyclopedia. McGraw-Hill. Film. Middle grades. $5.

How to Use Maps and Globes Series. McGraw-Hill. 6 filmstrips. Middle grades. $6.50 each.

It's Your Library. Mahnke. Film. 10 min. Primary through college. $55.

Know Your Library. Coronet. Film. 1 reel, 11 min. Junior and senior high school. Color, $120; b & w, $60.

The Language of Graphs. Coronet. Film. 13½ min. Intermediate through senior high school. Color, $120, b & w, $60.

Learning to Use Maps. Encyclopaedia Britannica. 6 filmstrips. Junior and senior high school. $6 each.

Library Organization. Coronet. Film. 1 reel, 11 min. Junior and senior high school. Color, $120; b & w, $60.

Library Series. McGraw-Hill. 6 filmstrips. Junior and senior high school. $25 per set; $4.50 each.
  The Books
  The Card Catalog
  The Dewey Decimal System
  The Dictionary, Part 1
  The Dictionary, Part 2
  The Encyclopedia

Library Tools Series. McGraw-Hill. 6 filmstrips. Junior and senior high school. $7 each.
  Aids in Writing and Reading
  Almanacs and Yearbooks
  Books for Biography
  Gazetteers and Atlases
  One-Volume Encyclopedias
  Readers' Guide to Periodical Literature

Look It Up. Coronet. Film. 1 reel, 11 min. Junior and senior high school. Color, $120; b & w, $60.

Maps and Their Use. Coronet. Film. 1 reel, 11 min. Junior and senior high school. Color, $120; b & w, $60.

Maps Are Fun. Coronet. Film. 1 reel, 11 min. Elementary through adult. Color, $120; b & w, $60.

Reading Maps. Encyclopaedia Britannica. Film. 11 min. Middle grades. Color, $120; b & w, $60.

Understanding a Map. McGraw-Hill. Film. 11 min. Intermediate. $60.

Use Your Library for Better Grades and Fun, Too. Society for Visual Education. Filmstrips. Grades 7 through 12. $6 each.

Using the Library. Encyclopaedia Britannica. 6 filmstrips. Junior and senior high school. $6 each.

We Discover the Dictionary. Coronet. Film. 1 reel, 11 min. Intermediate. Color, $120; b & w, $50.

What Is a Map? McGraw-Hill. Film. 11 min. Intermediate. $60.

Your Dictionary and How to Use It. Society for Visual Education. 6 filmstrips. Grades 4 through 6. $28.50 per set; $5 each.

Word Recognition

Basic Primary Phonics. Society for Visual Education. Filmstrips. Grades 1 through 3. $4 each.
  Group 1. 6 filmstrips. Grades 1 and 2. Initial consonant sound, seeing, saying, and hearing sounds.
  Group 2. 6 filmstrips. Grades 2 and 3. Blends; 2-letter sounds; 2- and 3-letter

sounds; combinations; final consonants; seeing, saying, and hearing sounds.

Group 3. 6 filmstrips. Grades 2 and 3. Short vowel, long vowel, etc.; seeing, saying, and hearing sounds.

Instant Words. Learning Through Seeing. 2 sets, 12 filmstrips each. Primary through senior high school. $30 per set.

Let's Pronounce Well. Coronet. Film. 1 reel, 11 min. Intermediate and junior high school. Color, $120; b & w, $60.

Pathways to Phonics Skills. American Book Co. 6 12-in. records. 33⅓ rpm. 3 albums. Grades 1, 2, and 3. $11.

Phonetic Analysis: Consonants. Pacific. Filmstrips. Primary and elementary. $20 per set; $6 each.

Phonetic Analysis: Vowels. Pacific. Filmstrips. Primary through junior high school. $35 per set; $6 each.

Phonics: A Key to Better Reading. Society for Visual Education. 6 filmstrips. Grades 3 through 6. $27.

Phonics: A Way to Better Reading. Society for Visual Education. Filmstrips. Grades 3 and 4. $5 each.
  Help Yourself Read
  Let's Start with Key Words
  Make Words Work for You
  Test Yourself on Sounds
  Vowel Sounds Help You
  Your Eyes and Ears Are Good Helpers

Phonics Practice. Learning Through Seeing. Filmstrips. Primary through senior high school. $30 per set.
  Set 1: *Vowel Sounds*
  Set 2: *Consonant Blends*

Practice in Phonetic Skills. Scott, Foresman. Filmstrip. Grades 1 through 3. $7.20.

Reading Development. Learning Through Seeing. 3 sets, 12 filmstrips each. Senior high school through adult. $36 per set.

Reading Improvement: Word Recognition Skills. Coronet. Film. 1 reel, 11 min. Junior and senior high school. Color, $120; b & w, $60.

Reading Records. Educational Recording Services. Records. Grades 1 through 3. $1.10 each.
  How to Learn the Foundation Words
  What Are the Foundation Words?

Riddle-A-Rhyme. Eye Gate House. 6 color filmstrips. Kindergarten through grade 3. $30 per set; $4 each.
  Consonants P, B, M, W, WH, F
  Consonants V, T, D, N, Y, H
  Consonants K, G, NG, NK, NGL, LK, KW, (Q), TW
  Consonants L, S, Z, R, BR, CR, DR, FR
  Consonants SH, CH, J, ZH, TH
  Consonant Combinations L and R
  Consonant S Combinations
  Vowels and Diphthongs

Seeing Skills. Learning Through Seeing. 2 sets, 12 filmstrips each. Elementary through senior high school. $30 per set.

Set B: Easier forms, letters, numbers
Set C: Complex forms, code groups

Sound Way to Easy Reading. Bremner-Davis. Records. Grades 1 through 3. $25 for series.

Sounds Around Us. Scott, Foresman. 3 records, 78rpm. Primary. $7.20.

Sounds for Young Readers. Educational Recording Services. Records. 3 albums. Kindergarten through grade 3. 98¢ each.

Steps to Mastery of Words. Educational Recording Services. Records. $20 per album.

What Are the Foundation Words? Educational Recording Services. Record. Primary. $1.10.

What's the Word? Houghton Mifflin. 12 filmstrips. Context, phonetic, structural analysis. $39 per set.

Word Study Skills. McGraw-Hill. 6 filmstrips. Middle grades. $7 each.

General

Beginning Responsibility: Books and Their Care. Coronet. Film. 1 reel, 11 min. Primary. Color, $120; b & w, $60.

A Book for You. McGraw-Hill. Film. 17 min. Junior high school. $105.

Choosing Books to Read. Coronet. Film. 1 reel, 11 min. Junior and senior high school. Color, $120; b & w, $60.

Defining the Good Reader. Coronet. Film. 1 reel, 11 min. Elementary through senior high school. Color, $120; b & w, $60.

Fundamentals of Reading. Eye Gate House. 9 color filmstrips. Kindergarten through grade 8. $30 per set.

How to Choose Books You Can Read. Educational Recording Services. Record. Primary. $1.10.

How to Choose Books You Like. Educational Recording Services. Record. Primary. $1.10.

It's All Yours. Teen Age Book Club. Film. 11 min. Elementary through adult. $50.

It's Fun to Read Books. Coronet. Film. 1 reel, 11 min. Intermediate. Color, $120; b & w, $60.

Let's Listen. Ginn. 3 10-inch records. 33⅓ rpm. 10 min. Reading readiness and speech development. $8.

Listening and Reading Skills. Society for Visual Education. Filmstrip. 39 frames. Junior and senior high school. $5.

Listening Time. Webster. 3 albums. Grades 1 through 3. $5.95 per album.

Listen Well, Learn Well. Coronet. Film. 1 reel, 11 min. Primary and intermediate. Color, $120; b & w, $60.

Reading Readiness. Encyclopaedia Britannica. 9 filmstrips. Primary. $6 each.

Materials for In-Service Training

The Audio-Visual Materials Consultation Bureau, Wayne University, Department of Language Education, College of Education, Detroit, Mich. 48202
  Gregory Learns to Read. Film. Color, $235; b & w, $135.
  Bel-Mort Films, 614 Cascade Bldg., Portland, Ore. 97204.

    Grouping Students for Effective Learning (filmstrip)
    Interpreting a Published Test (filmstrip)
    Instructional Materials (filmstrip)

Bureau of Audio-Visual Instruction, University of Iowa, Iowa City, Iowa 52240
    The Alphabet in Teaching Word Recognition. Film. 24 min. Rental, $4.50; sale, $75.
    News Time in First Grade Reading. Film. 22 min. Rental, $3; sale, $75.
    The Reading Period, Part I. Film. 33 min. Third-grade level. Color rental, $8.25, sale, $215; b & w rental, $4.50, sale, $110.
    The Reading Period, Part II. Film. 38 min. Third-grade level. Color rental, $11, sale, $225; b & w rental, $6, sale, $110.
    Teaching the Study Skills. Film. 28 min.
    Using a Reading Readiness Book. Film. 21 min. Rental, $3; sale, $75.

Educational Recording Services, 5922 Abernathy Dr., Los Angeles, Calif. 90045
    Building More Phonics Skills (R14, record, $1.10)
    Differences in Reading Ability (Emmett A. Betts, $6.90)
    The First Essential in Reading Improvement Providing for Individual Differences in the Classroom (Emmett A. Betts, $6.90)
    First Steps in Phonics (R13, record, $1.10)
    Improving Reading At All Levels (Marion Monroe, $6.90)

International Film Bureau, Inc., 332 S. Michigan Ave., Chicago, Ill. 60604
    They All Learn to Read. Film. 26 min. Third-grade level. Rental, $4.50; sale, $135.
    Why Can't Jimmy Read? Film. 15 min.

Learning Through Seeing, Box 368, Sunland, Calif. 91040
    High Speed Reading. Film. 8 min.
    Reading Improvement in the Secondary School. Film. 20 min.
    Reading Pacers. Film. 10 min.

McGraw-Hill Book Co., Inc., Text-Film Department, 330 W. 42d St., New York, N.Y. 10036
    Children Learn From Filmstrips. Film. 16 min. Color, $200 each; b & w, $105. All five purchased together: Color, $895; b & w, $470.
    Choosing a Classroom Film. Film. 18 min.
    Creating Instructional Materials. Film. 15 min.
    How to Use Classroom Films. Film. 15 min.
    Selecting and Using Ready-Made Materials. Film. 17 min.

Selected Catalogs and Source Books of Audio-Visual Materials

Colorado State College, Instructional Materials Center; and University of Colorado, Bureau of Audio-Visual Instruction. *General Film Catalog.* Boulder: University of Colorado.

Educational Film Guide. New York: H. W. Wilson Co. Cumulative editions and annual supplements.

Educators Guide to Free Films. Compiled and edited by Mary Foley Horkheimer and others. Randolph, Wis.: Educators Progress Service. Annual editions.

Educators Guide to Free Filmstrips. Compiled and edited by Mary Foley Horkheimer and others. Randolph, Wis.: Educators Progress Service. Annual editions.

5th U.S. Army, Signal Corps, Film and Equipment Exchange Services. *Army Films for Public Use.* Annual editions.

Filmstrip Guide. New York: H. W. Wilson Co. Cumulative editions and annual supplements.

Florida State University, Audio-Visual Center. *Educational Films.* Tallahassee: the University.

George Peabody College for Teachers, Division of Surveys and Field Services. *Free and Inexpensive Learning Materials.* Nashville, Tenn.: the College.

Indiana University, Division of University Extension, Audio-Visual Center. *Educational Motion Pictures.* Bloomington: the University.

Mountain Plain Film Library Association. *Joint Film Catalog and Supplements.* Boulder, Colo.: the Association.

National Education Association, Department of Audiovisual Instruction. *National Tape Recording Catalog.* Washington: the Association. Recent editions and supplements.

U.S. Office of Education, Department of Health, Education, and Welfare. *U.S. Government Films for Public Educational Use.* Washington: Government Printing Office. Recent editions.

University of Illinois, Division of University Extension, Audio-Visual Aids Service. *Catalog of Educational Films and Supplements.* Champaign: University of Illinois.

University of Utah, Extension Division, Audio-Visual Bureau. *Films for Better Teaching.* Salt Lake City: University of Utah.

University of Wisconsin, University Extension Division, Bureau of Audio-Visual Instruction. *Catalogue of 16 mm. Motion Pictures.* Madison: the University.

WITHAM, ANTHONY P. (ed.). "The Index to Reading Material," *Elementary English,* XL (May 1963), 546–52.

List of Publishers of Audio-Visual Materials

American Book Co., 55 Fifth Ave., New York, N.Y. 10003

Bailey Films, 6509 DeLongpre Ave., Hollywood, Calif. 90028

Bel-Mort Films, 614 Cascade Bldg., Portland, Ore. 97204

Bremner-Davis, 511 Fourth St., Wilmette, Ill. 60091

C-B Educational Films, Inc., 703 Market St., San Francisco, Calif. 94104

Coronet Films, 65 E. South Water St., Chicago, Ill. 60601

Educational Devices, Inc., 500 Fifth Ave., New York, N.Y. 10036

Educational Recording Service, 5922 Abernathy Dr., Los Angeles, Calif. 90045

Encyclopaedia Britannica Films, Inc., 1150 Wilmette Ave., Wilmette, Ill. 60091

Eye Gate House, Inc., 146-01 Archer Ave., Jamaica, N.Y. 11435

Ginn & Co., Statler Bldg., Back Bay P.O. 191, Boston, Mass. 02117

Houghton Mifflin Co., 2 Park St., Boston, Mass. 02107

The Jam Handy Organization, 2821 E. Grand Blvd., Detroit, Mich. 48211

Learning Through Seeing, Inc., Box 368, Sunland, Calif. 91040

McGraw-Hill Book Co., Inc., Text-Film Department, 330 W. 42d St., New York, N.Y. 10036

Mahnke Productions, Inc., 215 E. 3d St., Des Moines, Iowa 50309

Northwestern University Press, 816 University Pl., Evanston, Ill. 60201

Pacific Productions, Inc., 414 Mason St., San Francisco, Calif. 94102

Perceptual Development Laboratories, 6767 Southwest Ave., St. Louis, Mo. 63117

Popular Science Publishing Co., Inc., Audio-Visual Division, 355 Lexington Ave., New York, N.Y. 10017

Scott, Foresman and Co., 433 E. Erie St., Chicago, Ill. 60611

Society for Visual Education, Inc., 1345 W. Diversey Pkwy., Chicago, Ill. 60614

State University of Iowa, Bureau of Audio-Visual Instruction, Iowa City, Iowa 52240

Teen Age Book Club, Scholastic Book Services, 33 W. 42d St., New York, N.Y. 10036

University of Illinois, Visual Aids Service, Champaign, Ill. 61820

Webster Publishing Co., Division of McGraw-Hill Book Co., 1154 Reco Ave., St. Louis, Mo. 63126

Administrator, communication with: about in-service programs, **15;** about line and staff responsibilities, **13;** about special services, **15;** concerning schedules, **13–14;** on budget and plant facilities, **15;** on policies and practices, **15;** regarding mechanics of program, **13;** through reports, **15–16**

Bulletins, **9, 33–34, 52–54;** for community, **9;** for teachers, **33–34, 52–54**

Classroom organization: individualization, **28;** interest and research groups, **28;** interest centers, **85;** reading-level groups, **27;** reading-needs groups, **27;** use of an agenda, **84;** whole class as group, **27**

Committees, **7–8, 38, 68, 71–72;** for test construction, **71–72;** for test selection, **68;** reading, **38;** with adult and student representation, **7–8**

Community, communication with, **4–5, 9–11**

Community-school functions, **5–8**

Conferences, **6–7, 54;** helping teachers prepare for, **6–7;** points to remember, **7;** with teachers, **54**

Curriculum coordinators, **39–42;** getting help from, **42;** giving help to, **40–41;** relationships with, **39**

Demonstrations, **10, 11, 35–36, 50–52;** by consultant, **35–36;** for parents and other adults, **10;** for teachers, **50–52;** tips for preparation of, **11**

Department heads, **39–42;** getting help from, **42;** giving help to, **40–42;** relationship with, **39**

Directed Reading Lesson, **53**

Evaluation: appraising tools of, **68–71;** day-to-day, **26–27;** informal tools of, **71–75;** proper use of tools of, **25–26;** purposes for, **64–65;** selecting tools of, **25, 67–68;** standardized tools of, **66–67**

Experimentation, **36–37, 55**

Formal tests, **66–71;** *see also* Standardized tests; Testing; Tests

Grouping, **27–28**

Independent Activities: bibliography on, **95–96;** for grade 1, **85–89;** for grades 2 through 10, **89–95;** guide to development of, **84;** organization of classroom for, **84–85**

Informal Reading Inventory (IRI): administration of, **72;** construction of, **71–72;** criteria for scoring, **72–74**

Informal tests, **71–75;** *see also* Testing; Tests

In-service education: at specific times, **48–55;** demonstrations as part of, **35–36, 50–52;** formal courses as part of, **55;** guides for, **47–48;** materials for, **115–116;** of specific types, **48–55;** planning for, **15;** use of professional library in, **55–56**

Materials: bibliographies of, **97–105, 108–116;** criteria for selection and evaluation of, **80;** establishing a professional library of, **55-56;** for parents, **9;** instructional, **33;** professional, **33–34**

Minimum Standards for Professional Training of Reading Specialists, **23–24**

New approaches to reading instruction: color coding, **22;** *Initial Teaching Alphabet* (ITA), **17–18;** language-experience approach, **21–22;** linguistics, **18–20;** *The Montessori Method,* **20–21;** programed reading, **18**

Observations, **5, 34–36, 54–55;** by board members, **5;** by consultant, **34–35;** by teachers, **35, 36, 54–55**

Parents: bibliography for, **103–105;** committee membership of, **7–8;** communication with, **4–5, 9–11;** conferences with, **6–7;** kindergarten orientation for, **6;** materials for, **9;** suggestions for, **81–83;** teaching by, **6, 8**

Phonics, a sample lesson, **51–52**

Reports, **5, 15–16;** to administrator, **15–16;** to board of education, **5**

Research, formal, **37;** *see also* Experimentation

Special services, **15, 42–45**

Standardized tests, **66–71;** *see also* Testing; Tests

Summer programs, **8, 62–63**

Supervisors, **39–42;** getting help from, **42;** giving help to, **40–42;** relationship with, **39**

Testing, **58–60, 64–67, 71–74;** intelligence or capacity, **58–59, 67;** other factors, **59–60, 67;** purposes for, **64–65, 71;** reading ability, **58–60, 66;** use of IRI in, **71–74**

Tests, **25–26, 59–60, 67–71, 74–75;** administration and scoring of, **26, 69–70;** limitations and merits of standardized, **68–69;** selection of, **25, 67–68;** teacher-made, **74–75;** types of, **59–60, 71;** use of, **25–26**

Tips for reading consultants: checklist for consultants, **14;** conducting in-service programs, **48;** conducting meetings with specialists, **40;** conducting a workshop for teachers, **50;** consultant's observations, **35;** distributing bulletins, **54;** preparation of lesson demonstrations, **11;** preparation of reports to the board of education, **5;** research and experimentation, **37;** scheduling remedial instruction, **62;** teacher observations, **36;** test administration, **26**

Workshops, **50**